FLORIDA STATE
UNIVERSITY LIBRARIES

JUN 22 2001

TALLAHASSEE, FLORIDA

HOUSEHOLD CHOICE AND URBAN STRUCTURE

Household Choice and Urban Structure
A Reassessment of the Behavioral Foundations of Urban Models of Housing, Labor and Transportation Markets

PAUL A WADDELL

Ashgate
Aldershot · Brookfield USA · Singapore · Sydney

© Paul A. Waddell 1997

All rights reserved. No part of this publication may be reproduced, stored in a retrieval system, or transmitted in any form or by any means, electronic, mechanical, photocopying, recording or otherwise without the prior permission of the publisher.

Published by
Ashgate Publishing Ltd
Gower House
Croft Road
Aldershot
Hants GU11 3HR
England

Ashgate Publishing Company
Old Post Road
Brookfield
Vermont 05036
USA

British Library Cataloguing in Publication Data

Waddell, Paul A.
    Household choice and urban structure : a reassessment of
    the behavioral foundations of urban models of house, labor
    and transportation markets
    1. Sociology, Urban
    I. Title
    307.7'6

Library of Congress Catalog Card Number: 97-70637

ISBN 1 85972 526 0

Printed and bound by Athenaeum Press, Ltd.,
Gateshead, Tyne & Wear.

Contents

List of figures	vii
List of tables	viii
Acknowledgments	x
1 Introduction	1
2 Theoretical background: models of urban spatial structure	5
The gravity model	6
Other urban simulation models	14
Monocentric models	17
Discrete choice models	25
Ecological models	36
3 The policy interface	39
Transportation	40
Urban labor and housing markets	41
4 The region, the data, and the model	44
Geographic scope	45
Data	46
Model specification	53

5 Results and interpretation   **70**

    Model estimation results   70
    Model specification alternatives   81
    Interpretation of results   81

6 Conclusions and directions for future research   **109**

    Conclusions   109
    Directions for future research   115

Bibliography   **116**

List of figures

Figure	2.1	The binary probit model	28
Figure	4.1	The joint logit specification	61
Figure	4.2	2-level nested logit specification	63
Figure	4.3	3-level nested logit specification	64
Figure	5.1	Function of distance from Dallas CBD	84
Figure	5.2	Function of distance from Fort Worth CBD	84
Figure	5.3	Coefficients on job supply variables, by race	98
Figure	5.4	Travel time function from workplace to Dallas CBD	98
Figure	5.5	Travel time function from workplace to Ft. Worth CBD	99
Figure	5.6	Coefficients on wage variables, by race	102
Figure	5.7	Coefficients on workplace percent black	104
Figure	5.8	Coefficients on workplace percent hispanic	106
Figure	5.9	Disutility of travel in the journey to work	108

List of tables

Table 4.1	Cross-classification characteristics	50
Table 4.2	Characteristics for which means were calculated	52
Table 4.3	Characteristics of residential locations	56
Table 4.4	Characteristics of workers	57
Table 4.5	Characteristics of workplaces	58
Table 5.1	Variable definitions	72
Table 5.2	Model estimation results for 3-dimensional joint logit	74
Table 5.3	Model estimation results for 2-dimensional nested logit: residence / tenure / workplace	76
Table 5.4	Model estimation results for 3-dimensional nested logit: residence / tenure / workplace	78
Table 5.5	Summary measures of goodness-of-fit for estimated models	80
Table 5.6	Population density gradients	86
Table 5.7	Annual earnings by race (1979 $)	88
Table 5.8	Residential segregation in 1970 and 1980	90

Table	5.9	Workers by household type	93
Table	5.10	Housing tenure	95
Table	5.11	Educational attainment of workers	96
Table	5.12	Employment density gradients	100
Table	5.13	Wage gradients with respect to distance from the CBD	103
Table	5.14	Mean annual wages by educational attainment (1979 $)	104
Table	5.15	Mean travel time to work by income	108

Acknowledgments

Many individuals contributed to this work, though as always, any omissions or errors remain the responsibility of the author. I would like to thank Brian Berry for his stimulating intellectual support as the primary advisor for this research, John F. Kain for his probing and persistent encouragement, George Farkas for his early contributions to engaging my interest in some of the key questions examined here, Alex Anas for his feedback and scholarly work from which I drew heavily, Royce Hanson for his thoughtful support and confidence, and Phil Salopek, who made the data on which the research is based accessible.

1 Introduction

The last several decades have witnessed a massive reorganization of urban American society, including a dramatic dispersal of population and jobs from central cities, the rise of 'edge cities,' profound demographic and social changes such as the prevalence of dual-earner households and a shrinking middle class. Urban policy has not kept pace with these changes, and neither has our understanding of the complex interactions between market forces and public policy in shaping the evolution of cities and regions. Both the research on urban development and the public policies intended to shape it have devolved into piecemeal and often incoherent frameworks.

Population and employment have suburbanized rapidly during the four decades since World War II, with widespread declines in the population of central cities (Berry and Dahmann, 1977). Suburbanization has accelerated as a result of massive public investments in freeways, rising affluence among large sections of the population, and white flight from the central cities. The urban landscape has been reshaped by new suburban office corridors along sprawling expressways, far from the central business districts which once dominated the urban form. Manufacturing employment has stagnated, while service employment has grown dramatically, with heavy consequences for the occupational demands and opportunities for different segments of the population, and strong spatial implications as the new service jobs cluster in high rise office buildings in the central business districts and throughout the suburban sprawl.

New ethnic concentrations have formed in metropolitan pockets, and the black ghettoes in declining central cities have become a seemingly permanent fixture. The ghetto underclass has faced diminishing access to, and contact with, the remainder of the urban economy. Travel patterns have lost their suburb to downtown orientation, and been replaced by dispersed suburb to suburb, crosstown, and reverse-commuting patterns which frequently congest the beltways in the suburbs as much as the radial freeways emanating from the city center.

Suburbs have mushroomed and multiplied until they fragment the urban landscape and preclude further expansion of the central cities, limiting the capacity of central cities to compete for decentralizing jobs and households.

The urban labor market, the urban housing market, transportation policy and infrastructure, and individual and collective attitudes such as racial discrimination all interact to form a physical, economic, and social map of the metropolis. Perhaps one reason so many urban policies have failed in the past relates to their failure to address this systematic set of spatial interactions in an informed fashion, leading to fragmentary and incomplete, or worse - contradictory policies for urban development.

Similarly, the academic study of the urban environment has often failed to adequately integrate the relevant disciplines to focus on urban problems in a systematic manner. The models of urban dynamics which have been developed in the fields of urban economics and sociology have added significant insights into the nature of urban problems, but each provides only a partial perspective, and few adequately incorporate the spatial context in which urban processes transpire. Nor do current modeling efforts adequately describe public policy dimensions. Considering the degree to which the urban landscape is shaped by public investments, this is a serious shortcoming.

Several efforts have been made recently to cross disciplinary boundaries to attempt to develop quantitative urban models of the interactions between the labor market, housing market, transportation system, and public policy in a spatial context. While these tend to be well grounded in urban economic theory, there is a shift towards the implementation of such models using random utility theory, which is a stochastic extension of consumer economic theory. These models are typically operationalized with multinomial or nested logit formulations.

Among the more significant recent models of this type are the housing and tenure submodels of the Harvard Urban Development Simulation (HUDS) model described by Kain and Apgar (1985), and the Chicago Area Transportation and Land Analysis System (CATLAS) developed by Anas (1982). The HUDS model uses a multinomial logit model of the demand for bundles of housing attributes and neighborhood location for 96 different household types by racial, socioeconomic, and demographic category, given workplace location and travel costs. CATLAS develops a simultaneous equilibrium nested logit model of travel mode to work and residential location choice, given workplace and travel cost.

The model developed in this study is an attempt to extend this line of research by focusing on several related choices made by individual workers. The choice of a job given the location of firms, the choice of residence location given the spatial distribution of housing supply, the choice of housing tenure, and the choice of travel mode to work are all related decisions made by employed householders. These decisions can easily be seen to be related, but the exact nature and sequence of the decision making process is less clear.

The major urban models which were developed in the past several decades, including those developed from the monocentric model of Alonso (1964) and the Lowry (1964) gravity model, have assumed workplace to be exogenous in determining residential location. Hamilton (1982), however, has found that actual commuting distance is about eight times larger than would be expected from the monocentric model, indicating a large degree of 'wasteful commuting'. One of the main reasons for this result, according to Hamilton, is that residential relocation costs are significant, and may in many cases lead to workplace location decisions being made from predetermined residential locations.

Similarly, Linneman and Graves (1983) have argued that 'job search and residence decisions are intimately intertwined over both short and long distances', and Weinberg (1979) that individuals can adjust accessibility by adjusting workplace location or residence location or both. Simpson (1980,1986) has extended these arguments by estimating a simultaneous equation model of residence and workplace location using microdata for Toronto. Although individuals would not be expected to make simultaneous decisions regarding their residence and workplace locations (Gordon and Vickerman, 1982), some individuals will make workplace decisions based of predetermined residence location while others make residence decisions on the basis of predetermined workplace locations.

The degree to which residence location is driven by workplace location, or the converse, may also vary by household relationship, tenure, ethnicity, and socioeconomic status. Beesley and Dalvi (1974) have argued that residential choice is primarily the decision of the household head, with the likely implication that secondary workers in the household choose their workplace on the basis of a predetermined residential location. Homeowners face higher relocation costs than renters, and would be expected to be more likely than renters to choose their workplace on the basis of their residential location. To the extent that blacks face discrimination in housing choice, their residential location opportunities are restricted, and they are more likely to be forced to choose a job based on their residential location. Schwartz (1973) has found that more educated workers adopt a larger job search radius, confirming that higher socioeconomic status confers greater flexibility in the choice of both residential and workplace location.

This study uses multinomial and nested logit modeling as tools to examine this interdependent decisionmaking process in detail, for white, black, and Hispanic workers. The resulting model of the choice of workplace location, residence location, housing tenure, and travel mode provides a more systematic view of the interrelationships between, and spatial aspects of, labor supply, housing demand, and transportation service demand. The public policy areas impacted by these areas include transportation and land use planning, housing, labor, economic development, and racial discrimination.

The model is estimated using a special tabulation prepared by the U.S. Census Bureau Division of Journey to Work and Migration specifically for this study, using 1980 data for the Dallas-Fort Worth SMSA. The data contains detailed commuting patterns and housing choices by travel mode, and by detailed racial, demographic, and socioeconomic worker categories.

2 Theoretical background: models of urban spatial structure

Several strains of theoretical development are relevant to the objectives of this research, and will be discussed at some length in this chapter. Although this background only skims the surface of the vast literature which exists in these areas, it will suffice to provide a foundation to pursue a strand of research which integrates several of these branches of research. The principal components to be discussed in this chapter are 1) the development and extension of urban simulation models, particularly gravity models, 2) the monocentric model of urban economic theory, 3) random utility theory and discrete choice modeling, and 4) social and urban ecology.

The development of theoretical and quantitative models of the spatial characteristics of the urban housing and labor markets, and the resulting pattern of intraurban commuting, has evolved along many diverse channels. The land-use forecasting models developed as inputs to the transportation planning process are perhaps the most widely implemented models of urban spatial activity. Most of these models are grouped into a class of models known as gravity models, and have been employed more for their computational tractability than their underlying theoretical foundations. These models have been stretched to include more elements of household behavior, but are still often criticized for their lack of a solid foundation in behavioral theory.

Other urban simulations have been developed to analyze a variety of issues related to urban spatial structure, including several housing market models with a high degree of household and housing detail and some spatial detail. Typically, these models are better rooted in urban economic theory than the gravity models, but tend to be designed for special purpose applications and are extremely complex.

The field of urban economics has developed over the past twenty years a rigorous theoretical foundation for urban modeling, beginning with the insights of Alonso (1964). The early urban economic model of Alonso was extended by Muth (1969), Mills (1967), and others into what has come to be known as the monocentric model of the city. This model, and its extensions, have yielded a wealth of insight into the spatial dimensions of urban economic activity through a solid grounding in economic theory. The urban economic models require assumptions, however, which reduce significantly their theoretical and empirical applicability.

The development of a theory of random utility, assimilating microeconomic principles and discrete choice theory, has provided the potential for developing urban models which are more realistic, and more tractable to estimate empirically. Developed initially in the field of psychology by Luce and Suppes (1965), random utility theory soon gained ground in transportation planning in application to travel mode choice analysis. In transportation planning applications, McFadden (1973), Ben-Akiva (1973), and Domencich and McFadden (1975) developed the multinomial and nested logit models. Recently, Anas (1981), Quigley (1976), Lerman (1977), and McFadden (1978) have begun to explore the potential for applying multinomial and nested logit models of discrete choice to not only mode choice, but also to the choice of residential location. Anas (1982) has perhaps gone the farthest in developing a general equilibrium model of housing demand, housing supply, and travel mode.

In the following sections, the main elements of these channels of development will be summarized, beginning with the development of various urban simulation models, particularly gravity models, and proceeding with the primary concepts and applications of urban economics and random utility theory.

While there are scores of urban simulation models which have been developed to date, one group of these models which has achieved the most widespread implementation in land use and transportation planning is the gravity model and its derivatives. The next section will focus on the evolution of these models, and other urban simulation models will be briefly reviewed subsequently.

The gravity model

Geographers and other social scientists have often attempted to describe the regularities of the spatial distribution of population activities by borrowing analogies from the more mathematically rigorous and deterministic physical sciences. The consistent empirical observation that the level of human interaction tends to vary inversely with increasing distance has been frequently used by geographers as justification for the application of the Newtonian concept of gravitational force to the explanation of human behavior in a spatial context. This analogy has come to be known as the gravity model of spatial interaction.

The early work by Stewart (1942), Dodd (1943), Isard (1960), and Lowry (1964) led to the development of what has come to be known as the Lowry model, or more generally the gravity model. This early work provided a convenient quantitative analogy which appeared consistent with the aggregate behavior of population, but lacked theoretical grounding. The lack of a theoretical foundation has been the chief criticism of the gravity model throughout its use in the past several decades. Yet despite this weakness, the gravity model has come into widespread use in recent years, particularly in land use and transportation planning applications.

Isard (1960) and Lowry (1964), followed by Wilson (1973) and Putman (1983), pioneered the practical use of the gravity model for residential location predictions for metropolitan planning, primarily for transportation planning. Crecine (1964) was the first to use the Lowry framework in developing an operational forecasting model called the Time Oriented Metropolitan Model (TOMM), which he developed for the Pittsburg Community Renewal Study. This effort was never completed, but was documented well by Brewer (1973).

Goldner (1968, 1972) was more successful in implementing Lowry's framework in an operational forecasting model. He developed the Projective Land Use Model (PLUM), which incorporated several improvements to Lowry's original formulation, and provided incremental, rather than single-year solutions. This model was later modified by Putman (1976) as DRAM (Disaggregated Residential Allocation Model).

Within the history of the gravity model's development, there have been repeated efforts to endow the original deterministic model with a theoretical basis. Isard (1960) and Huff (1961) began using a probabilistic framework to replace the deterministic nature of the Newtonian gravity concept. Wilson (1973) reformulated the Lowry model using the concept of entropy, which in physics describes the tendency of systems to move towards the most disordered state. Wilson used the entropy framework to find the most probable distribution of home-to-work trips, in a manner which provided an internal consistency and mathematical tractability previously missing from gravity model applications, and which was consistent with statistical mechanics. This reformulation made it easier to introduce into the model complications which could be interpreted behaviorally.

Other researchers who operationalized the Lowry model included Garin (1966) and Batty (1971). By incorporating Wilson's contributions on entropy maximization, Batty and Mackie (1972) focused on improvements to the calibration procedures for this class of models, which had generally been ad-hoc and iterative procedures previously. Putman (1976) stated that "in U.S. practice, with but one exception, no Lowry type model has ever been successfully calibrated (in a statistical sense)". The exception to which Putman referred was the Urban Growth Simulation Model (UGSM), developed by A.M. Voorhees and Associates (1972) for the North Central Texas Council of Governments.

Among the most significant extensions and operational applications of the Lowry class of gravity models is the development of the Integrated

Transportation and Land Use Package (ITLUP) by Putman (1980, 1983). This set of models was significant not only for the improvement in behavioral content, but also not because it was the first successful integration of land use and transportation models. Putman disaggregated persons in the model by income quartile, and included the income distribution of an area as predictive variables, as well as land use characteristics such as the amount of residential land and its density. The ITLUP model system includes DRAM for residential allocation, and EMPAL, for employment allocation. DRAM assumes a distribution of workplaces, and predicts residence location based on the accessibility to workplace and a set of residence attractiveness variables. EMPAL predicts employment location based on a lagged distribution of workers, access to residents, and a set of workplace attractiveness variables.

The ITLUP model system has been tested in numerous metropolitan areas, and provide the most extensive behavioral foundation for the Lowry gravity class of models to date. Their application for transportation planning, however, with iterative calibration procedures used to estimate these models on trip end data rather than actual trip matrices, and the lack of a rigorous economic theoretical foundation, pose limitations for potential use in empirically testing behavioral theories of residence and workplace location.

A brief review of the development of the gravity model and its structure follows. The discussion is intended to provide a foundation for comparison to the deterministic models developed in urban economics and to the models which have begun to evolve from random utility theory.

The original Lowry model

The original Lowry specification of the gravity model was the first practical application of the gravity analogy to the problem of predicting urban locations. Borrowing on the physical law of gravity as a computational analogy, Lowry used two assumptions: first, employment location determines residential location (ceteris paribus), and second, the propensity to travel decreases with increasing distance.

The implementation of these assumptions took the form

$$p_{ij} = d_{ij}^{-1.33} \qquad \textbf{2.0}$$

where p_{ij} is the probability of commuting from zone i to zone j, d_{ij} is the distance from zone i to zone j, and $d_{ij} >= 1$

This formulation implies simply that there is an exponentially declining propensity to commute as commuting distance increases. The specific value of the exponent of -1.33 was empirically estimated by Lowry. For the purposes of our discussion, the equation will be generalized to

$$p_{ij} = d_{ij}^{-\beta} \qquad \text{2.1}$$

To complete the Lowry model specification, the total number of persons living in zone i is predicted by

$$N_i = g \sum_j E_j p_{ij} \qquad \text{2.2}$$

where N_i is the number of persons living in zone i, E_j is the number of employees working in zone j, and g is a scale factor.

Within this model specification, the scale factor g adjusts for labor force participation rates, unemployment rates, and workers per household ratios, as well as scaling the totals to a regional total number of persons. Although this scale factor assures that at the regional level, the total number of persons by the model is consistent with a desired total, it cannot ensure consistency between the input number of employees by zone and the implicit prediction of zonal employment when the predicted trips from all residence zones to each workplace zone are summed. This is because the scale factor is regional rather than zone specific.

Entropy maximization

Lowry's model was reformulated by Wilson (1973) using the entropy maximizing principle, another analogy drawn from physics. The entropy maximizing work of Wilson led to the solution of the inconsistencies inherent in the original gravity model by replacing the regional adjustment factor (g) with an array of balancing factors:

$$B_j = \left(\sum_i c_{ij}^{-\beta} \right)^{-1} \qquad \text{2.3}$$

Equation 2.1 can now be rewritten as

$$p_{ij} = B_j c_{ij}^{-\beta} = \frac{c_{ij}^{-\beta}}{\sum_j c_{ij}^{-\beta}} \qquad 2.4$$

by substitution, equation 2.2 becomes

$$N_i = \sum_j E_j B_j c_{ij}^{-\beta} = \sum_j E_j \left(\frac{c_{ij}^{-\beta}}{\sum_i c_{ij}^{-\beta}} \right) \qquad 2.5$$

This revised form of the model preserves both the desired regional population totals as well as the original zonal employment totals.

Model extensions

Several extensions to the gravity model were made after Wilson's entropy formulation. Some of the more significant extensions are reviewed briefly here, including alternative travel functions, the creation of multivariate zonal attractiveness terms, and model disaggregation for different household types.

A second extension of the basic Lowry model was the consideration of alternative trip functions to the negative exponential form in the original model. Putman (1983) examines the use of the modified gamma function as a more realistic view of travel behavior. The property of this form is that travel propensity rises with increasing distance over a short distance, and then decays rapidly as distance increases past a break point. This pattern of trip making is almost universally observed, since opportunities for work or shopping increase with increasing distance, while the desire to travel decreases with increasing distance. The form of this alternative trip function is as follows:

$$f(c_{ij}) = c_{ij}^{\alpha} e^{(-\beta c_{ij})} \qquad 2.6$$

The principal criticism of the gravity model to date has been the lack of a theoretical foundation for its implementation, and its simplistic use of an analogy drawn from physics. While the early uses were intended for predictive application in land use modeling, and were indeed somewhat deserving of such criticism, one particular extension of this basic framework has transformed it into a useful framework for behavioral analysis. This important extension is the incorporation of a residential attractiveness term which could be used to measure socioeconomic and land use influences on residential location. The attractiveness term is incorporated by separating the probability term in equation 2.4 into an attractiveness component, W_i, and a trip function component, $f(c_{ij})$:

$$p_{ij} = \frac{W_i f(c_{ij})}{\sum_i W_i f(c_{ij})} \qquad 2.7$$

This specification also has the property of preserving the balancing factor (2.3) by the form of the denominator. The general form of such a multivariate attractiveness measure could be:

$$W_i = f\left(X_{i1}^{\alpha_1}, X_{i2}^{\alpha_2}, X_{i3}^{\alpha_3}, \ldots, X_{i\epsilon}^{\alpha_n}\right) \qquad 2.8$$

where X_{ik} are zonal attributes, and α_k are empirically derived parameters. Putman (1983) has done extensive testing with one such function, of the form

$$W_i^g = \prod_k X_{ik}^{\alpha_{gk}} \qquad 2.9$$

where W_i is a measure of the attractiveness of zone i to resident type g, X_{ik} is the kth attribute of zone i, and α_{gk} are empirically estimated parameters.

Note that the form of equation 2.9 adds not only a multivariate attractiveness index, but also allows for the disaggregation of persons into separate types. This combination of extensions changes the nature of the gravity model from a simple physical analogy into a flexible framework for analyzing the residential location behavior of different groups, and examining the separate influences of a variety of zonal characteristics. In order to disaggregate the model in this manner, the model would be calibrated separately for each person type.

The resulting form of the model after extensions to incorporate a multivariate attractiveness component and person type disaggregation is the following:

$$N_i = \sum_j E_j \left(\frac{\prod_k X_{ik}^{\alpha_{gk}} c_{ij}^{\alpha} e^{(-\beta c_{ij})}}{\sum_i \prod_k X_{ik}^{\alpha_{gk}} c_{ij}^{\alpha} e^{(-\beta c_{ij})}} \right) \qquad 2.10$$

Model calibration

As described by Putman (1983), calibration means the adjustment of the parameters in the equations of a model so as to maximize the goodness of fit between the estimate of a particular variable in the model and the observed value of that variable, both for the same base time period. Most of the early residential location models were based on linear equations, and could be calibrated via the usual least squares procedures. Other nonlinear location models were calibrated with curve-fitting procedures, or often with repetitive trial and error procedures.

The implementation of residential location models based on entropy-maximizing principles and incorporating multivariate travel decay functions and attractiveness terms has led to the development of new calibration procedures. Of particular relevance is the usual unavailability of spatial interaction data, defining the residence-workplace commuting flows by household and employment type. This latter constraint precludes the use of standard calibration methods.

The calibration of an attraction-constrained residential location model as described in equation 2.0 has been tested using several different criteria for measuring goodness of fit. The coefficient of determination, or R^2 statistic, is frequently used as a measure of goodness of fit. Since the model takes a multivariate nonlinear form, the R^2 response surface is used to search for the best fit parameters. R^2 is calculated as follows:

$$R^2 = 1 - \frac{\sum_i (\hat{N}_i - N_i)^2}{\sum_i (N_i - \overline{N})^2} \qquad 2.11$$

where N_i is the observed number of employed residents in zone i, $\hat{N}_i$ is the estimated number of employed residents in zone i, and $\overline{N}_i$ is the mean of N_i.

The use of the R^2 as the criterion for guiding the calibration procedure involves an iterative search procedure on the partial derivative of the R^2 with respect to each of the parameters in the model. Through iterative search programming techniques, the global minima and maxima of these partial derivatives can be found.

One problem with the R^2 statistic as a criterion for a gradient search procedure is that it has been shown to be very flat in the range of the optimum values of the parameters. Extensive testing by Putman (1983) and others indicates that it is not very sensitive to changes in the parameters in the range of the optimum. As a result of this insensitivity, other measures of goodness of fit have been developed for use as the search criterion in calibration.

A second criterion, L, which has been used to measure of goodness of fit is a log-likelihood function:

$$L = \sum_i N_i \ln p(\hat{X}_i) \qquad 2.12$$

where

$$p(\hat{X}_i) = \left(\frac{\hat{N}_i}{N_i}\right) \qquad 2.13$$

is the probability of observing $\hat{N}$ in zone i, $\hat{N}$ is the estimate of the employed residents in zone i, and N_i is the observed number.

One property of this log-likelihood function is that for a perfect fit between the observed and estimated values of N_i the value of L equals zero. The calibration procedure, as with the R^2 criterion, involves an iterative gradient search of the partial derivative of this log-likelihood function with respect to each of the parameters in the model.

The advantage of L over R^2 as a criterion to guide the search procedures for calibration is that the shape of the response surface in the range of the optimum is much more peaked, so that a maximum or minimum is more pronounced at the optimal point, and the gradient search is therefore more efficient. This criterion is also one of the only available options when only the trip end data are available.

In testing by Putman (1983), however, it was found that this criterion was a function of the specific data set used in calibration, thus making comparison between calibrations on different data sets invalid. A second limitation of calibrating an attraction-constrained residential location model with the available procedures is that it is difficult, if not impossible, to derive statistical significance tests on the individual parameters in the model.

In order to make comparison of results more feasible between data sets, a third criterion has been developed based on the likelihood function and calculated in a manner analogous to the R^2. Called the best/worst ratio, or φ, it is designed to measure the improvement that the best-fit parameters provide above the worst-fit parameters.

In order to construct this criterion, the 'best' and 'worst' likelihood values are calculated. The worst likelihood value corresponds to an equiprobable distribution of employed residents, so that the estimate of employed residents in each zone equals the mean value across all zones:

$$L_w = \sum_i X_i \ln[p(\overline{X})] \qquad 2.14$$

The best likelihood value corresponds to the estimate in each zone exactly equal to the observed number of employed residents:

$$L_b = \sum_i X_i \ln[p(X_i)] \qquad 2.15$$

Combining these terms in a form similar to the R^2, the best/worst ratio is calculated:

$$\phi = 1.0 - \frac{L - L_b}{L_w} \qquad 2.16$$

This ratio ranges from values close to zero for extremely poor fit calibrations to 1 for perfect fit results, as does the R^2 value.

To summarize the criterion functions described here, the likelihood function L is used to guide the search procedure for the best fit parameters, and the best/worst ratio is used for comparison between calibration of different data sets.

While these calibration procedures have been tested extensively by Putman and others and have been generally found to be robust, they are nevertheless somewhat limited in two ways: first, they do not produce measures of statistical significance on individual parameters, and second, they are somewhat sensitive to starting parameters and local minima and maxima.

Other urban simulation models

Land use models

One of the earliest attempts to develop a systematic model of urban land use patterns was the Chicago Area Transportation Study, CATS (1960). This effort, and the related work of Hamburg (1960), and Hamburg and Creighton (1959), used an extensive historical database for Chicago on floor area, population densities, and vacant land, to develop a model based on development capacity.

CATS began a period of substantial activity in the development of applied urban location models. Most of the subsequent models can be grouped into gravity models, discussed above, and econometric models, of which the major models will be summarized here.

Much early attention was devoted to the use of linear programming to develop urban location models. Among the most notable of these attempts was the work by Harris (1962) and Herbert and Stevens (1960) in support of the Penn-Jersey study. At the time, a linear programming implementation could not be completed due to a variety of complications including computer limitations. A prototype model was eventually developed by Harris (1966) and Wheaton (1974). The Herbert-Stevens model, as it has come to be known, has not actually been used in an operational study of land use forecasting, but has influenced several later studies, including Senior (1977), and two housing market models which incorporated elements of its linear programming framework: the NBER Urban Simulation Model [Kain, Apgar, and Ginn (1977a,b)], and the Harvard Urban Simulation (HUDS) model [Kain and Apgar (1985)].

One of the more widely used residential and employment location forecasting models of an econometric nature is EMPIRIC, developed by Hill (1965, 1966) for the Boston area transportation study. The model has received substantial criticism due to its weak theoretical foundation, but has been implemented in several metropolitan areas, including Boston, Atlanta, Denver, Puget-Sound, Minneapolis-St. Paul, and Washington D.C. [Peat, Marwick, and Mitchell (1972)]. EMPIRIC is a linear, simultaneous equation system designed to predict changes in shares of regional population and employment. It is based heavily on lagged dependent variables, therefore capturing little economic behavior and relying heavily on the persistence of land use patterns. Most of the metropolitan areas which have used the model have since dropped it in favor of one of the gravity models such as DRAM/EMPAL, or other more ad-hoc procedures.

Housing market models

Several models have been developed to analyze the effects of housing policies on the behavior of the housing market. These models are significant because of the degree to which they are based on economic theory, and implement partial of general equilibrium models of the housing market. The earliest of this class of models was developed by Little (1966) for the San Francisco Community Renewal Program. The ADL model, as it was known, was given a detailed and critical review by Brewer (1973). The model was concerned principally with the housing market in the central city, and was designed to address a variety of housing and community development policies, rather than forecasting residential location.

The San Francisco model was criticized for, among other things, failing to take into account competition between the housing market in the central city and that of the suburbs. The model did, however, disaggregate households into 114 types defined by income, family size, race, and age. Dwelling units were disaggregated into 27 types by structure type, tenure, number of rooms, and condition, and the housing market was disaggregated geographically into 106 neighborhoods. The model was also significant because it assumed profit maximizing behavior by housing suppliers, and explicitly incorporated projected rents, and estimates of the cost of new construction and renovation.

The Urban Institute (UI) model was developed by Deleeuw and Struyk (1975) to study numerous housing and development policies including housing allowances [Vanski (1976) and Marshall (1976)], the Section 8 program, public housing, interest rate subsidies for new construction, and the Section 312 Rehabilitation Loan program [Ozanne and Vanski (1980)]. Improvement to computational efficiency and relaxation of several constraints was made by MacRae (1982), and the model's conceptual foundation was extended, partly through use of microdata from the Annual Housing Survey, by Struyk (1983). The model simulates the housing market and obtains end of decade market clearing prices and quantities in a manner that represent long run equilibrium solutions. The model uses 25 to 45 model households to represent the housing and population of Chicago during 1960-1970, and uses six geographic zones to represent the Chicago metropolitan housing market.

The most comprehensive and complex of the housing market models is the series of econometric models beginning with the National Bureau of Economic Research (NBER) model of the Detroit housing market [Ingram, Kain, and Ginn (1972)]. The model was revised and used to evaluate the market effects of housing allowances [Kain, Ginn, and Apgar (1977), Kain and Apgar (1977)], and revised again to evaluate the impacts of geographically focused housing improvement programs [Kain and Apgar (1981), Kain and Apgar (1985)]. The third version is known as the HUDS model, or Harvard Urban Development Simulation model.

Although it is similar in some respects to the Urban Institute model, the HUDS model introduces significant additional detail in almost every aspect, adding substantially to its complexity. The model is estimated in the Chicago area from a random sample of 72,000 to 85,000 households and dwelling units, and divides the metropolitan area into almost 200 zones. Housing is represented as a multidimensional bundle of three types of housing services: structure type, neighborhood quality, and housing quantity at a given location. Although both the UI and the HUDS models use a housing services production function, the HUDS model separates the housing services accruing from the dwelling from those due to the quality of the neighborhood, and incorporates more explicitly expectations about future rents and costs, and neighborhood quality.

The demand sector of the HUDS model is based on a multinomial logit function in which 96 types of households grouped by race, age, headship status, family size, and income choose between 50 types of housing bundles defined by five neighborhood quality levels and ten structure types on the basis of the relative minimum gross prices of the bundles. These gross prices are the sum of a dwelling unit's market rent and the commuting costs a household would incur to consume a particular type of housing in a particular zone.

Also of note, the HUDS model explicitly incorporates the effects of racial discrimination by adding to the utility function of white households terms not only for wealth and employment accessibility, but also for racial preference, and by calibrating these simultaneously. This reflects the assumption that whites prefer to live in neighborhoods with higher proportions of white residents. The model assumes blacks are indifferent about the racial composition of their neighborhoods.

Monocentric models

Historical development

The field of urban economics has evolved over the past two and one half decades from the seminal work of Alonso (1964), who developed a mathematical model of urban land use that remains central to current urban economic theory. Early work in this field centered on bid rent theory, and through the influence of Muth (1969), Mills (1972), and others, a robust 'monocentric model' of the urban landscape was developed. The model was based on the utility maximizing behavior of households, and was therefore rooted in consumer economic theory.

In a simple monocentric model of firm location, Mills (1984) assumes a single profit maximizing industry, a single export node at the central business district (CBD), and no households or labor inputs to produce the result of a land rent and density gradients which are steeper near the center of the city. In a parallel simple model of household location, Mills assumes a homogeneous utility maximizing population, with all jobs located in the CBD, spatially constant housing construction costs, and substitution of land and capital in the production of housing services to generate the result of a land rent and density gradients which are steeper near the center of the city.

In extensions of this simple formulation of the monocentric model, Mills (1984) and others allow multiple industries, multiple housing types, competition for locations between firms and households, and even for some relaxation of the assumption that all employment occurs in the CBD. The model becomes more realistic as these assumptions are relaxed, and actually produces results which are consistent with empirical evidence in terms of several aspects of urban form. The monocentric model demonstrates, for example, why almost all land near the CBD tends to be used by firms rather than households and why population density falls at a decreasing rate as distance from the CBD increases. It has been shown to provide relatively accurate predictions on the behavior of density, land rent, and housing prices, and helps to explain the trend towards decentralization which has occurred in recent decades as transportation costs have declined.

The monocentric model has some severe limitations which reduce its applicability and realism, however. On of the most important of these limitations is that, although some allowances have been made for limiting the assumption that all employment locates in the CBD, location is a one dimensional variable in the model: distance from the CBD. The model is therefore incapable of handling the now common circumstances of large suburban employment centers. The strength of the monocentric model has been its ability to generate analytical results. According to Mills, this analytical strength would be greatly diminished if two dimensional location were incorporated, due to the inordinate mathematical complexity which would be required.

One of the principal hypotheses embedded in the monocentric model is the housing cost - transportation cost tradeoff. Also known as the gross price hypothesis, this holds that households maximize their total utility by choosing the highest utility combination of commuting and housing. Higher income households are hypothesized to live farther from the center of the city than poor households, since their increase in utility from greater housing consumption outweighs their decreased utility from increased commuting costs as their income rises, which is a function of the income elasticity of these two items. As a secondary result of these preferences, higher income households outbid lower income households for suburban land, causing lower income households to consume less land and locate closer to the center of the city in housing which is higher density and more expensive per square foot.

Although the monocentric models are partial equilibrium models, more complex general equilibrium models have been developed by Mills (1967), Dixit (1973), and others which simultaneously analyze the employment, housing, and transportation sectors of the urban economy. One of the most complete general equilibrium models of this type was a linear programming model developed by Mills (1972b), and extended by Hartwick and Hartwick (1974) and Kim (1979). These extended models need not be restricted to monocentric assumptions, and are therefore better able to handle more realistic urban forms.

The field of urban economics has provided a powerful analytical foundation for the analysis of urban spatial residential and workplace location patterns, commuting patterns, and the spatial behavior of the urban housing and labor markets. In spite of this robust theoretical foundation, however, Anas (1982) has noted that urban economic theory has not yet been extensively incorporated in the fields of urban simulation modeling and transportation planning, which are more empirical in nature. The reason, Anas suggests, is that a stochastic implementation of urban economics is preferred for empirical analytical tasks.

He proposes that the emerging field of random utility theory could serve effectively to implement urban economics in a stochastic formulation more amenable to empirical analysis. In addition, there are classes of problems which can be characterized as discrete choice problems, with which the calculus of urban economics cannot as easily cope.

Residential bid rent

While the origins of bid rent analysis lie in von Thhnen's (1966) model of agricultural land use, the urban economic models developed in the 1960's by Muth (1969) and Mills (1967) combine the bid rent approach with neoclassical economics. This section reviews the residential bid rent model, following the notation used by Anas (1982) in his summary of bid rent analysis.

The bid rent approach to the residential market can be viewed as an auction, with households submitting bids for housing or locations, and housing or land owners auctioning land or housing off to the highest bidder. The approach assumes that both consumers and suppliers have perfect information about the market. The following assumptions regarding the urban environment and consumer behavior also apply. The shape of the city is circular, with all employment located at the center. Each household has one worker, who is employed at the CBD and commutes there daily from the residential location of the household. Land outside the CBD is owned by absentee landlords who can allocate their land to either agricultural or residential use, and agricultural bids for land are identical at all locations. All housing is assumed to be identical and infinitely durable, differing only in location and size of lots. Landowners choose the profit maximizing use of their land between agricultural and residential uses, and the profit maximizing size of parcels to subdivide their land for sale.

The result of these assumptions is that at each location there are a set of bid rents by households representing their willingness to pay for a house of a given lot size at each location, and a set of asking rents by landowners at each location. For equilibrium, it is assumed that the bid rent equals the asking rent, each parcel of land is allocated to the highest bidder, each household must be indifferent among different locations, each household must be able to find a location within the city, and both residential and agricultural bid rents equal the asking rent of landowners at the edge of the city. For stationarity, it is assumed that exogenous economic variables affecting the residential market remain unchanged over time, each household's annual income and its tastes remain unchanged over time, and the costs of transportation, the price of agricultural land, and the total household population remain constant. The stationarity assumptions allow all costs, prices, and incomes to be stated either in annual values or as the present value of a stream of annual values.

The utility function of each household can be represented as

$$U = U(Z, Q), \text{ with } \frac{\partial U}{\partial Z}, \frac{\partial U}{\partial Q} > 0, \qquad 2.17$$

where Q is the lot size of a dwelling, and Z is the income of a household allocated to all expenditures other than housing and transportation. If U, Q, and Z are allowed to vary over distance from the CBD, the formulation can be generalized to

$$U(x) = UZ(x), Q(x). \qquad 2.18$$

The budget constraint of the household can be expressed as

$$Y - Z(x) - R(x)Q(x) - T(x) = 0, \qquad 2.19$$

where Y is the household's income, T(x) represents the commuting costs to and from the CBD, and R(x) is the rent paid by the household per unit of land. Since each household has fixed income and commuting costs, and must take the rent at a given location as fixed, the consumer choice problem is

$$\max_x \{\max_{Z,Q} U(Z, Q|x) \text{ subject to } Y - Z - R(x)Q(x) - T(x) = 0\} \quad 2.20$$

Bypassing the derivation (shown in Anas (1982), pp. 21-22), the inner maximization provides the demand functions for Z and Q at each location x, written as

$$Z^*(x) = Z[Y - T(x), R(x)],$$
$$Q^*(x) = Q[Y - T(x), R(x)]. \qquad 2.21$$

The outer maximization equated to the choice between alternative locations, at each of which the optimal combination of Z and Q have already been chosen. This function is written as

$$\max_x U[Z^*(x), Q^*(x)]. \qquad 2.22$$

The incomes and tastes of all households are assumed to be identical, leading to the same location x^* being chosen by all households. The choice is conditional on land rent, however, so landowners at other locations will lower their rents in order to attract households to alternative locations. The landowner's rent maximization problem can be stated as

$$\max_{Q} \overline{R}(x,Q) = \frac{Y - T(x) - Z[\hat{U}(x), Q]}{Q}, \qquad 2.23$$

where $\hat{U}(x)$ is the utility of location x anticipated by the landowner. The result of the landowner's supply decision is a supply function of the size of the lots to be supplied at x, given the household's net income $T - T(x)$ and the anticipated utility level $\hat{U}(x)$. This supply function can be expressed as

$$Q^*(x) = \hat{Q}[\hat{U}(x), Y - T(x)]. \qquad 2.24$$

Long run equilibrium in stationary conditions results from the interaction of the households' and landowners' maximization functions in a bidding process. The resulting land rent gradient, (bypassing the derivation shown in Anas (1982), pp. 23-26) can be stated as the following differential equation

$$\frac{dR(x)}{dx} = -\left[\frac{dT(x)}{dx}\right]Q^{-1}, \qquad 2.25$$

which indicates that the land rent gradient is negative with respect to distance from the CBD. Given the assumption that land is a normal good, households of higher income will demand more land at location x than poorer households.

Generalizing the model to include consumption, lot size, and travel time to the CBD, the household's utility expression becomes

$$U = U(Z, Q, t) \quad \text{with} \quad \frac{\partial U}{\partial t} < 0, \qquad 2.26$$

where t is the household's commuting time. The household faces not only a budget constraint, but also a time constraint. At equilibrium conditions, the land rent gradient becomes

$$\frac{dR}{dx} = -\left[\frac{dT}{dx} - \left(\frac{\partial U/\partial t}{\partial U/\partial Z}\right)\frac{dt}{dx}\right], \qquad 2.27$$

indicating that the equilibrium land rent gradient, as before, must decline with distance. Assuming land as a normal good, if households are separated into two classes by income levels, then $Q^*(x)_2 > Q^*(x)_1$, and $(dR/dx)_2 > (dR/dx)_1$. The steeper rent gradient for poor households indicates that poor households will outbid wealthy households for centralized locations, assuming identical tastes. If utility functions are allowed to vary by income class, the bid rent function of the wealthy may still be flatter than that of the poor, but only if the increase in utility from a larger lot farther from the CBD is larger than the decrease in utility from increased travel time at that location. Under these conditions, the monocentric model produces the analytic result that wealthy households will tend to live farther away from the CBD than poor households.

Racial prejudice

Race has received substantial attention as an influence on urban spatial structure throughout the development of the field of urban economics. Mills and Price (1984) conducted an empirical study of the effects of central city problems such as crime, taxes, and large minority concentrations on the suburbanization of population and employment. They found that only minority population showed a significant influence on population and employment density gradients. Mills (1985) went farther, to conclude that the integration of the suburbs should slow or reverse the suburbanization of jobs, and that stricter enforcement of open housing laws would therefore benefit central cities.

Race has been explicitly incorporated into urban economic models in various ways. Bailey (1959) originated what have been called border models of racial prejudice. The border model has been extended by Muth (1969, 1975), Courant (1974), Rose-Ackerman (1975), and Courant and Yinger (1977). Bailey's original model assumed complete segregation, and that whites prefer to live away from blacks, and that blacks prefer to live near whites. These conditions lead whites to pay more for housing in the white interior than near the black-white border, and blacks to pay more for housing near the border than in the black interior. Competitive conditions in the market are then expected to lead to the sale of properties near the border by whites to blacks, or by blacks to whites, until the price is equal on both sides of the border. This leads to the highest prices in the white interior, and the lowest prices in the black interior.

Muth (1975) argued that border price differentials were the most likely reason for segregation, even though there was little empirical evidence of the price effects. He argued that alternative explanations of racial segregation, such as discrimination by landlords and real estate agents, was unlikely, since discriminating entities would be driven out of business by competition from entities which did not discriminate: "...if competition among nondiscriminating landlords and agents eliminates excess profits for them, discriminators, whose costs are higher relative to revenues, would tend to lose money and be forced out of business."

Yinger (1975) incorporates racial prejudice into the monocentric model of Alonso (1964), Muth (1969), and Mills (1967) by assuming that the racial composition of a location affects a household's utility, and by deriving, for both whites and blacks, the rent-distance functions reflecting racial composition. The rent-distance functions imply that if whites prefer segregation and some blacks prefer integration, then there exists no stable locational equilibrium without the presence of discrimination. In essence, neighborhood stability is seen as a public good which can be purchased with discrimination. This conclusion, of course, directly contradicts the argument made by Muth, that such discrimination would be eliminated by competition.

The lack of a stable locational equilibrium without discrimination implies that as enforcement of anti-discrimination laws becomes more effective - that is, as overt discrimination decreases - as long as the underlying white prejudice is not removed, the result will be an accelerated filtering of the housing stock. Prejudiced whites, unable to prevent the invasion of their neighborhoods by minorities through discriminatory practices, would be more likely to flee their neighborhoods, relinquishing them to upwardly mobile minority residents. As Berry (1976) has observed in the Chicago housing market, the filtering of housing tends to be accelerated under conditions of rapid growth in the housing stock at the periphery of the metropolitan area. It is expected that tight housing markets would be more likely to show higher levels of discrimination and slower housing filtering, while soft housing markets would tend to reduce the frequency of housing discrimination, and increase the pace of filtering of the older, more central housing stock from whites to minorities, and from higher income to lower income.

Courant and Yinger (1977) reject the border models of Bailey (1959) and Muth (1969, 1975), arguing that border models are logically inconsistent without unrealistic assumptions regarding either the relative incomes of blacks and whites, or the extent of white prejudice. And Yinger (1979), summarizing the evidence on the role of race in urban spatial structure writes:

> The evidence reviewed...overwhelmingly supports the proposition that racial discrimination is a powerful force in urban housing markets. Only a theory that involves discrimination can explain why blacks are concentrated in a central ghetto, why blacks pay more for comparable housing in the same submarkets, why prices of equivalent housing are

higher in the ghetto than in the white interior, and why blacks consume less housing and are much less likely to be homeowners than whites with the same characteristics. The evidence of discrimination, based on recent data, makes a convincing case for government intervention in the housing market.

The approaches taken by Muth, Courant, Rose-Ackerman, and Yinger, while significantly different from each other, are all based on the monocentric model. The structure of the monocentric model expresses space in one dimension: distance from the city center. This implies a symmetrical view of residential (or employment) location, with blacks occupying a central ring from distance u^0 at the city center to u^*, at the black-white border, with whites residing in the doughnut shaped ring from u^* to the edge of the city. While these extensions of the monocentric model provide useful analytical results, the one dimensional spatial representation required by the calculus of the monocentric model is an unrealistic representation of the asymmetrical pockets of racial concentration which are found in most urban areas, and limits the applicability of the models.

Residential and workplace choice

In the development and extension of the monocentric model, as with most other models of residential location, the determination of workplace has been assumed to be exogenous. This assumption has begun to come under increasing scrutiny, and several approaches have been taken to allow for the endogenous determination of workplace choice as well as residential choice.

Hamilton (1982) examined the predictive ability of the monocentric model in estimating the mean commuting time in urban areas. He found that the monocentric model overpredicts the actual level of commuting by a factor of eight. He calculated the level of commuting which would result from a random choice by households of both residences and workplaces, without any effort to economize on commuting, and found that this approach overpredicted the actual level of commuting by only 25 percent. In addition, the suburbanization of jobs, moving them closer to residences, has not resulted in the expected decrease in commuting, but rather to a slight increase. Hamilton concludes:

> ...these findings can hardly be taken as a ringing endorsement of the behavioral assumptions underlying the monocentric model. Something is wrong with a model when the predictions are off by a factor of eight and an assumption of random behavior has good predictive power.

Siegel (1975) has extended the monocentric model to allow households to simultaneously choose residential and workplace location, using a sample of households from the San Francisco Bay area stratified by housing tenure, race, and position in life-cycle. Simpson (1980, 1987) has also developed a model of simultaneous workplace and residential location choice, first in the Greater London area, and subsequently in the Toronto metropolitan area. Simpson grounds his model of workplace choice in two principles of spatial job search. The first principle is that, ceteris paribus, workers prefer jobs which are closer to their residential location. Simpson cites the human capital migration model of Greenwood (1975), and the job search model of McCall (1973) and Lippman and McCall (1976) in support of this principle. The second principle Simpson uses in his job search formulation is that skill acquisition broadens the spatial extent of the job search, citing Becker's (1964) work on specialization and the spatial extent of the labor market. In summarizing the rationale for incorporating the choice of workplace into models of residential location, Simpson (1987) writes:

> We simply do not know which individuals made residential locations last from cross-sectional travel-survey data, which are typically the only microdata available. The simultaneous model simply asserts, then, that workplace and residential location decisions are interdependent in the analysis of urban spatial structure and that our data do not permit us to analyze workplace and residential location decisions sequentially.

Both Siegel and Simpson attempt to model jointly the choice of residential and workplace location by extending the framework of the monocentric model. The difficulty with attempting to use the one dimensional calculus of the monocentric model to represent the relationship between residential and workplace location is obvious, however: the location of workplaces and residences are both measured with respect to the city center - not with respect to a two dimensional system of polar coordinates, or to each other. The relationship between residence and workplace cannot, therefore, be established. We must assume, in essence, that although neither workplace nor residential location are required to be at the city center, both residence and workplace must lie in the same direction from the city center for the distance between them to be known. This is an even stronger assumption than the assumption of a symmetrical distribution of residential locations required by the traditional monocentric model. Again, the calculus of the monocentric model provides a severe constraint on the practical application of the model.

Discrete choice models

The development of urban economic theory has been based heavily on the assumptions implicit in economic consumer theory, which describes a consumer as choosing a consumption bundle of commodities and services whose quantities are assumed to be nonnegative continuous variables. The assumption of continuous nonnegative quantities in consumer theory is necessary to allow the use of calculus to derive demand functions.

In the case of choice alternatives which are discrete choices rather than continuous variables, however, such as the choice of residential location, travel mode, or housing tenure, the optimization techniques of calculus cannot be used to derive demand functions. A different analytical approach, termed discrete choice theory, is required to analyze such circumstances. Discrete choice theory is consistent with consumer theory in assuming a rational consumer. The principal difference between the two is that choice theory works directly with the utility functions rather than deriving demand functions.

In examining the behavior of individuals making discrete choices, the field of psychology made pioneering steps in developing probabilistic choice theory. Luce and Suppes (1965) found experimental observations of inconsistent and nontransitive preferences, and introduced the probabilistic choice mechanism to explain these deviations from the expected choices. Two alternative interpretations of the probabilistic choice mechanism were made by Luce and Suppes (1965). The first argues that consumer behavior is inherently probabilistic, and the second argues that consumer behavior is inherently deterministic, but that analysts have incomplete knowledge of the decision processes of consumers.

These alternative interpretations lead, respectively, to constant utility and random utility approaches. The constant utility approach hypothesizes that the utilities of alternatives are fixed. In the random utility approach developed by Manski (1973), four sources of randomness are identified: unobserved attributes, unobserved taste variations, measurement errors and imperfect information, and instrumental variables. In both approaches, decisionmakers are assumed to choose the utility-maximizing alternatives.

To operationalize random utility theory, three steps are required:

1 Total utility is separated into deterministic and random components

$$U_{in} = V_{in} + \varepsilon_{in} , \qquad \textbf{2.28}$$

where V_{in} is the systematic, or deterministic component of the utility of alternative i for individual n, and ε_{in} is the random component of the utility.

2 The deterministic component is specified, using available hypotheses regarding the factors influencing the utility function,

and the computational efficiency of estimating the unknown parameters in the utility function. The balancing of these two criteria has generally led researchers to use specifications which are linear in the parameters.

3   The random component is specified. Ben-Akiva and Lerman (1987) have shown that the random components of utility functions can be assumed to have zero means, since any nonzero means of the disturbances are "absorbed" into the systematic components of the utility function. Depending on which assumptions are made regarding the nature of the random components of the utility functions, several different models can be derived, including the linear probability model, the probit model, and the logit model.

The simplest assumption regarding the distribution of the random components of utility is that the difference between disturbances of two alternatives is uniformly distributed between two fixed values -L and L, with L>0. This assumption generates the linear probability model, which has a linear probability function between -L and L, but has kinks at these two points. The discontinuity of this function presents theoretical difficulties which are better addressed by probit or logit models.

The binary probit model is based on the assumption that the disturbances are the sum of a large number of unobserved but independent components. By the central limit theorem, the distribution of these disturbances would be expected to be normal. In the probit formulation, the choice probabilities asymptotically approach zero and one, but never take on these values, as the systematic components of utility between alternatives diverge. Although the assumption of independent and normally distributed disturbances in the binary probit model are more realistic than the linear probability model, it is inconvenient analytically since the choice probability must be expressed as an integral. The binary probit model takes the form

$$P_n(i) = \Phi\left(\frac{V_{in} - V_{jn}}{\sigma}\right), \qquad 2.29$$

where $\Phi()$ denotes the standardized cumulative normal distribution, and σ is the standard deviation of the normal distribution of $\varepsilon_{jn} - \varepsilon_{in}$. Since $1/\sigma$ is the scale of the utility function, which can be set to an arbitrary positive value, it is generally assumed to be 1.

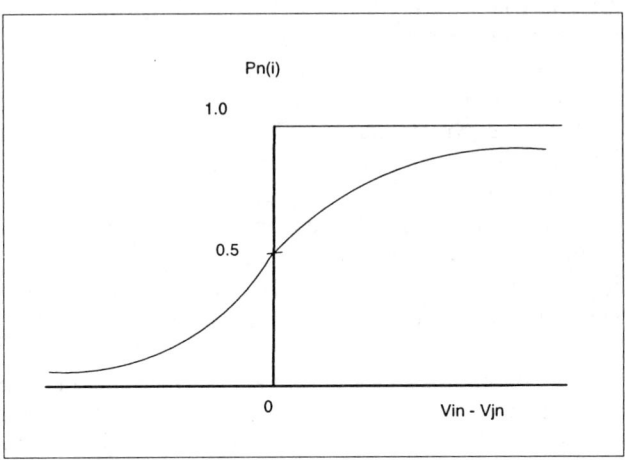

Figure 2.1 The binary probit model

The binary logit model is based on similar assumptions as the binary probit model, but is more convenient analytically. The random components of the utility function, $\varepsilon_n = \varepsilon_{jn} - \varepsilon_{in}$ is assumed to be logistically distributed:

$$f(\varepsilon_n) = \frac{1}{1+e^{-\mu\varepsilon_n}}, \quad \mu > 0, \quad -\infty < \varepsilon_n < \infty. \qquad 2.30$$

where μ is a positive scale parameter.

Although this function approximates the normal distribution, it has "fatter" tails.

The binary logit model has the form

$$P_n(i) = \frac{1}{1+e^{-\mu(V_{in}-V_{jn})}}. \qquad 2.31$$

Ben-Akiva and Lerman (1987) indicate that in the case of linear-in-parameters utilities, the parameter μ cannot be distinguished from the overall scale of the β's, and is therefore generally assumed to be 1 for convenience. In subsequent notation, therefore, it will be omitted for clarity.

The Gumbel distribution

The assumption of a Gumbel distribution of the disturbance terms forms the basis for the derivation of the multinomial and nested logit models which will be specified in later sections. Considerable detail regarding the properties of this distribution is presented here, and in the following two sections the derivation of the multinomial and nested logit models are presented. Proofs of the properties of the Gumbel distribution may be found in Johnson and Kotz (1970) and Domencich and McFadden (1975). Ben-Akiva and Lerman (1987) have noted that the assumption of Gumbel distributed disturbance terms in the multinomial logit model is equivalent to an assumption of a logistic distribution of ε_n in the binary logit model.

If ε is Gumbel distributed, then

$$f(\varepsilon) = \exp\left[-e^{-\mu(\varepsilon-\eta)}\right], \quad \mu > 0, \qquad 2.32$$

and

$$f'(\varepsilon) = \mu e^{-\mu(\varepsilon-\eta)} \exp\left[-e^{-\mu(\varepsilon-\eta)}\right], \qquad 2.33$$

where η is a location parameter and μ is a positive scale parameter. As summarized by Ben-Akiva and Lerman (1985), the Gumbel distribution has the following properties:

1. The mode is η.
2. The mean is $\eta+\gamma/\mu$ where γ is the Euler constant.
3. The variance is $\pi^2/6\mu^2$.
4. If ε is Gumbel distributed with parameters (η,μ) and V, and $\alpha>0$ are any scalar constants, then $\alpha\varepsilon+V$ is Gumbel distributed with parameters $(\alpha\eta+V,\mu/\alpha)$.
5. If ε_1 and ε_2 are independent Gumbel-distributed variates with parameters (η_1,μ) and (η_2,μ) respectively, then $\varepsilon^*=\varepsilon_1-\varepsilon_2$ is logistically distributed:

$$F(\varepsilon^*) = \frac{1}{1+e^{\mu(\eta_2-\eta_1-\varepsilon^*)}}. \qquad 2.34$$

6   If ε_1 and ε_2 are independent Gumbel distributed with parameters (η_1,μ) and (η_2,μ), respectively, then max $(\varepsilon_1,\varepsilon_2)$ is Gumbel distributed with parameters

$$\left(\frac{1}{\mu}\ln\left(e^{\mu\eta_1}+e^{\mu\eta_2}\right),\mu\right).\qquad 2.35$$

7   As a corollary to proposition 6, if $(\varepsilon_1,\varepsilon_2,\ldots,\varepsilon_J)$ are J independent Gumbel-distributed random variables with parameters $(\eta_1,\mu),(\eta_2,\mu),\ldots,(\eta_3,\mu)$, respectively, then max $(\varepsilon_1,\varepsilon_2,\ldots,\varepsilon_J)$ is Gumbel distributed with parameters

$$\left(\frac{1}{\mu}\ln\sum_{j=1}^{J}e^{\mu\eta_j},\mu\right).$$

The multinomial logit model

As an extension of the binary logit model to the more general case in which the choice set C_n consists of more than two alternatives, the multinomial logit model has the form

$$P_n(i)=\frac{e^{V_{in}}}{\sum_{j\in C_n}e^{V_{jn}}},\qquad 2.36$$

where C_n is the feasible choice set for individual n.

Ben-Akiva and Lerman (1985) derive the multinomial logit from the properties of the Gumbel distribution of the disturbance terms in a manner similar to Domencich and McFadden (1975). Their derivation is included here for reference in later sections. For convenience, Ben-Akiva and Lerman assume $\mu=0$ for all the disturbances, and order the alternatives so that $i=1$, then

$$P_n(1)=\Pr\left[V_{1n}+\varepsilon_{1n}\geq\max_{j=2,\ldots,J_n}\left(V_{jn}+\varepsilon_{jn}\right)\right].\qquad 2.37$$

Define

$$U_n^* = \max_{j=2,\ldots,J_n}\left(V_{jn} + \varepsilon_{jn}\right). \qquad 2.38$$

From property 7, U_n^* is Gumbel distributed with parameters

$$\left(\frac{1}{\mu} \ln \sum_{j=2}^{J_n} e^{\mu V_{jn}}, \mu\right).$$

Using property 4, U_n^* can be written as $U_n^* = V_n^* + \varepsilon_n^*$, where

$$V_n^* = \frac{1}{\mu} \ln \sum_{j=2}^{J_n} e^{\mu V_{jn}} \qquad 2.39$$

and ε^* is Gumbel distributed with parameters $(0,\mu)$.

Since

$$\mathbf{P}_n(1) = \Pr\left(V_{1n} + \varepsilon_{1n} \geq V_n^* + \varepsilon_n^*\right) = \Pr\left[\left(V_n^* + \varepsilon_n^*\right) - \left(V_{1n} + \varepsilon_{1n}\right) \leq 0\right], \qquad 2.40$$

by property 5 we have that

$$\mathbf{P}_n(1) = \frac{1}{1 + e^{\mu\left(V_n^* - V_{1n}\right)}} \qquad 2.41$$

$$= \frac{e^{\mu V_{1n}}}{e^{\mu V_{1n}} + e^{\mu V_n^*}} \qquad 2.42$$

$$\mathbf{P}_n(1) = \frac{e^{\mu V_{1n}}}{e^{\mu V_{1n}} + \exp\left(\ln \sum_{j=2}^{J_n} e^{\mu V_{jn}}\right)} \qquad 2.43$$

$$= \frac{e^{\mu V_{1n}}}{\sum_{j=1}^{J_n} e^{\mu V_{jn}}} \; . \qquad\qquad 2.44$$

The IIA property

One property of the multinomial logit model which has received much attention in the literature is the independence from irrelevant alternatives, or IIA property. This follows from the assumption that the disturbance terms are independent, which requires that any two alternatives not share unobserved attributes. The significance of the IIA property in application of the multinomial logit model is that under circumstances in which certain alternatives share unobserved attributes, the model will yield incorrect results.

The most classic example of this IIA problem is known as the red bus/blue bus paradox. In this example, there are three alternative modes of travel originally: blue bus, rail, and car. A fourth mode is added for red buses, identical in every facet to the blue buses except in color. Under these conditions, the multinomial logit model will predict a shift in ridership proportions to the red bus mode not only from the blue bus mode, but also from the car and rail modes, which should remain unaffected.

The IIA property becomes a problem only if the specification of the alternatives in the multinomial logit model includes alternatives which share unobserved attributes, and therefore have correlated disturbance terms. Specification tests have been devised by Hausman and McFadden (1984), to identify whether this problem exists in a particular specification.

The joint logit model

A further extension of the multinomial logit model is the case in which the choice set is complex, or has more than one dimension. For example, an individual might choose housing tenure and housing location, either in a simultaneous or a sequential manner. This two dimensional choice set can be represented as

$$C_n = C_{tn} \times C_{dn} - C_n^*, \qquad\qquad 2.45$$

where C_n is the full choice set for individual n, C_{tn} is the choice of tenure alternatives, C_{dn} is the choice of residential location alternatives, and C_n^* is the subset of C_n which is infeasible for individual n.

In multidimensional choice sets, it is possible that some of the observed attributes of elements in the choice set are shared across subsets of alternatives, or that some of the unobserved attributes are shared. In the event that the shared attributes are observed, a joint logit model is used. If, on the other hand, the shared attributes are unobserved attributes, a nested logit model is used.

In the example above, the utility expression can be written as

$$U_{dt} = V_d + V_t + V_{dt} + \varepsilon_{dt} \quad \forall (d,t) \in C_n, \qquad 2.46$$

where

V_d = the systematic component of utility common to all elements of C_n choosing destination d,

V_t = the systematic component of utility common to all elements of C_n choosing tenure t,

V_{dt} = the remaining systematic component of utility specific to the combination (d,t),

ε_{dt} = the random utility component

If the ε_{dt}'s are independently and Gumbel distributed across alternatives and populations, the multinomial logit model can be used for the joint choice of residential location and tenure:

$$P_n(d,t) = \frac{e^{V_t + V_d + V_{dt}}}{\sum_{(t,d) \in C_n} e^{V_t + V_d + V_{dt}}} . \qquad 2.47$$

The nested logit model

In the joint logit model, the elements of the multidimensional choice set share only observed attributes. If this restriction is relaxed so that elements of the multidimensional choice set may share both observed and unobserved attributes, a nested logit model is used.

The nested logit model was first developed as an extension of the joint logit model by Ben-Akiva (1973), and was subsequently formalized based on utility maximization by Daly and Zachary (1979), Williams (1977), Ben-Akiva and Lerman (1979), and McFadden (1978). The following assumptions of the nested logit model, and its derivation, are from Ben-Akiva and Lerman (1985).

Using the previous example, the utility expression becomes

$$\mathbf{U}_{dt} = V_t + V_d + V_{dt} + \varepsilon_t + \varepsilon_d + \varepsilon_{dt}, \qquad 2.48$$

where ε_t and ε_d are the unobserved components of utility attributable to tenure and destination choice, respectively, and ε_{dt} is the remaining unobserved component of random utility.

Assume:

1. Either ε_d or ε_t has zero variance. In the present example, let $\varepsilon_d = 0$.

2. ε_t and ε_{dt} are independent for all $d \in D_n$ and $t \in T_n$, where D_n and T_n are the marginal choice sets of destination and tenure choice, respectively.

3. The terms ε_{dt} are independently and identically Gumbel distributed with the scale parameter μ^d.

4. ε_t is distributed so that $\max_{d \in D_{nt}} U_{dt}$ is Gumbel distributed with scale parameter μ^m.

Ben-Akiva and Lerman (1985) show that only the ratio of the scale parameters μ^t / μ^d can be identified from the data, which makes it possible to normalize one of them to equal one.

Using these assumptions, Ben-Akiva and Lerman (1985) derive the nested logit model for the marginal choice probability as

$$\mathbf{P}_n(t) = \Pr\left(\max_{d \in D_{nt}} U_{dt} \geq \max_{d \in D_{nt'}} U_{dt'}, \; \forall t' \in T_n, \; t' \neq t \right) \qquad 2.49$$

$$P_n(t) = \frac{e^{(V_t + V'_t)\mu^t}}{\sum_{t' \in T_n} e^{(V_{t'} + V'_{t'})\mu^t}} \cdot \qquad 2.50$$

and the conditional choice probability as

$$P_n(d|m) = \Pr[U_{dt} \geq U_{d't}, \; \forall d' \in D_{nt}, \; d' \neq d \,|\, t \; chosen] \qquad 2.51$$

$$P_n(d|m) = \frac{e^{(V_{dt} + V_d)\mu^d}}{\sum_{d' \in D_{nt}} e^{(V_{d't} + V'_d)\mu^d}} \cdot \qquad 2.52$$

Discrete choice models of urban spatial structure

Multinomial and nested logit models have now been applied to many of the issues addressed by the housing and urban location models discussed earlier. The early development and application of these models related to the choice of travel mode, and included studies by McFadden (1973), Ben-Akiva (1973), and Domencich and McFadden (1975).

More recent research activity has included numerous additional applications to mode choice, but also to residential location. Such analyses include research by Quigley (1976) to analyze the demand for housing by rental households in Pittsburg using a multinomial logit model, and by Apgar and Kain (1974) to estimate housing submarket demand equations for renters and owner-occupants in the Chicago and Pittsburg housing markets. Lerman (1977) and McFadden (1978) developed multinomial logit models of residential destination choice, Anas (1981) estimated a multinomial logit model of joint residential location and travel mode choice, and as noted earlier, the housing demand and tenure choice components of the HUDS housing market simulation are also based on multinomial logit formulations [Kain and Apgar (1985)].

Stochastic equilibrium models using logit analysis were developed for traffic network equilibration by Daganzo and Scheffi (1977) and Scheffi (1978), and for rental housing market equilibrium by Anas (1980). Simulation models based on stochastic choice formulations of demand, used to study the impact of land use and transportation policies on real estate values were developed by Anas (1979) and Anas and Lee (1982). The CATLAS model developed by Anas (1982) is an attempt to integrate land use and transportation models for the Chicago metropolitan area using Census Journey to Work data from 1970, and additional travel time and cost data from the Chicago Area Transportation Study (CATS).

Anas has done much to reconcile the development of random utility theory and discrete choice modeling with two of the mainstream currents of urban spatial modeling discussed in this chapter: the monocentric model and the gravity model. Anas (1987) formulates a model of urban spatial structure for a monocentric city using a multinomial logit framework, and allowing for the presence of random tastes in an otherwise homogeneous population. His analysis goes a long way towards reconciling the monocentric model with the multinomial logit model, and revealing the opportunity for extending the analyses allowed by the monocentric model through a stochastic choice framework which circumvents many of the limitations of the calculus of the monocentric model. Anas (1981) also compared the multinomial logit model to the gravity model, and proved that the two approaches are identical in that the multinomial logit model can be derived and identically estimated by either method. He also proved that the doubly-constrained gravity model of Wilson (1967) is the same as a multinomial logit model of joint origin-destination choice, consistent with stochastic utility maximization.

By identifying the underlying similarity between the gravity model, the monocentric model, and the multinomial logit model, Anas has opened the door to research which synthesizes the best of these three approaches into a more robust and realistic approach. The discrete choice framework, further, allows us to integrate the theories of urban ecology, covered in the following section, with the analytical and quantitative rigor of urban economics.

Ecological models

The ecological approach to the study of urban social an spatial organization dates to the work of Park (1916). Borrowing many concepts from the field of ecology, such as competition, invasion, succession, and concepts of territory, the "ecological school" became a significant force in shaping urban spatial research both in sociology and geography, applying these concepts to the assimilation of waves of immigrants to the United States. This approach was reformulated by Hawley (1950), and came to be known as 'human ecology'.

The classical ecological model of Park (1916), Cressey (1938), and McKenzie (1968) describes the assimilation process as a new population group, distinct racially or ethnically from the established group, 'invade' the natural area occupied by the established group. The invasion areas are typically central areas surrounding the central business district, and the process evolves to one of 'succession' as the new group replaces the previously established group. In the classical model, the displaced population is typically of higher socioeconomic status than the incoming population, and relocates farther from the city center. Neighborhoods may experience numerous instances of invasion and succession as new waves of immigrants arrive in an urban area.

Early spatial descriptions of the patterning of population were provided by Hurd (1903), who identified axial and central growth patterns related to neighborhood characteristics such as income. Subsequently, Burgess (1925) developed a concentric zone model of urban structure which was based on the concepts of the ecological model: invasion and succession by lower status groups at the city center, and the resulting expansion of a low status concentric zone, and the outward movement of higher status residents to newer housing in concentric zones at the periphery of the urban area. Hoyt (1939) focussed on the axial pattern of development in his sectoral model of urban growth. This approach identified asymmetrical status differences which give rise to axial wedges of growth extending outward from the city center, and differentiated by socioeconomic status.

Berry and Kasarda (1977) summarize the results of a large number of factor analytic studies conducted since the Second World War, indicating that these two concepts of urban spatial pattern, combined with patterns of residential racial segregation which follow neither the concentric zone nor the sectoral pattern, have been well established as additive elements to the current view of urban structure:

> In each of these studies the answer is the same: there are three dominant dimensions of variation. These are (1) the axial variation of neighborhoods by socioeconomic rank; (2) the concentric variation of neighborhoods according to family structure; and (3) the localized segregation of particular ethnic groups.

Among the first to quantify the ecological model were Duncan and Duncan (1957), by classifying census tracts using data from two consecutive censuses into a sequential process beginning with initial 'penetration' by blacks, and advancing progressively to 'invasion', 'consolidation', 'and 'piling up'. The process implied an irreversible evolution, and indeed, there is little empirical evidence to contradict such an assessment. Taueber and Taueber (1965), in their classical <u>Negroes in Cities,</u> further extended this quantitative framework, analyzing a large number of cities from 1940 to 1960. Additional empirical support for the classical model, developed and applied extensively in Chicago, has been widespread, including research on Cleveland, Boston, and Seattle by Guest and Weed (1976), several southwestern cities by Massey (1981a, 1981b), and Detroit, St. Louis, and Cleveland by White (1984).

Gordon (1964) described seven steps in the assimilation process: acculturation, structural, marital, identificational, behavioral receptional, attitudinal receptional, and civic assimilation. Massey (1984) has argued that spatial assimilation is an essential step, once acculturation is accomplished, before structural assimilation and the remaining steps can proceed. Massey cites the importance of residential proximity for such variables as friendship, prejudice, and marriage. Several studies have documented the association between socioeconomic advancement and spatial mobility, including Lieberson (1963), Nelli (1970), Ward (1971), Thernstrom (1973), Esslinger (1975), Kobrin and Goldscheider (1978), and Burstein (1981).

In comparing the assimilation patterns of blacks and Hispanics in seven metropolitan areas in the southwest, Massey (1984) finds that black segregation is greater than that of Hispanics, and is less affected by factors such as socioeconomic status, suburbanization, and generation. Massey found that 77 percent of the census tracts in these SMSAs had at least 250 Hispanics, but only 27 percent of these tracts had more than 250 blacks. Black invasion areas were found invariably on the periphery of established areas, whereas Hispanic invasion areas were dispersed throughout the cities. Hispanic invasion was found to be much less likely to be followed by Anglo population loss than was invasion by blacks. Finally, for both blacks and Hispanics, social status was found to be positively related to distance from an established area, but blacks were found to have a lower ability to achieve separation from established areas.

In attempting to explain the discrepancy between black and Hispanic assimilation patterns, Massey states:

> It is not blacks that contradict our theory of spatial assimilation, but Anglos. Increasing black social status does not reduce the social distance that Anglos perceive between themselves and blacks. Areas of potential black settlement are restricted to tracts adjacent to existing black neighborhoods, and entry of blacks into these areas is almost always followed by residential succession, no matter what the objective socioeconomic characteristics of the entering blacks. In a sense, the ghetto follows upwardly mobile blacks as they attempt to assimilate spatially. As a result, they are less able to convert status attainment into spatial assimilation with Anglos.

3 The policy interface

The demand for residential location, workplace location, travel mode, and housing tenure form an interrelated web of household decisions which determine much about the fabric of the urban environment. Public policies are affected by these decisions in a variety of different ways, and in turn, influence these household decisions. Transportation systems are designed to accommodate peak hour journey to work patterns which are determined by the relationship between residences and workplaces. In turn, new transportation investments and varying congestion levels influence the demand of each household for residence and workplace locations. Similarly, a host of public policies have been developed to improve economic conditions in central city ghettoes, and to stem white flight to the suburbs. The decentralization of jobs in the post war era has led to unresolved policy debates between pursuing economic development within the ghetto, or increasing efforts to disperse the ghetto and improve the access of the poor to suburbanizing opportunities. The failure to effectively enforce open housing laws in most urban areas has been criticized as a major contributor to continued racial residential segregation. And in spite of equal employment opportunity laws, the gap in earnings and employment rates between whites and nonwhites have not diminished significantly.

The policy issues of transportation, housing, economic development, and discrimination are interrelated through the household's choices of residential and workplace location, travel mode, and housing tenure. A model of these dimensions of the household decisionmaking process has direct relevance, therefore, for each of these policy areas. In fact, a thorough analysis of these household choices calls for an integrated assessment of the influence of these public policy dimensions.

Transportation

In the postwar era, a massive national investment in intra-urban highways has reshaped the economies and form of most cities in the U.S. The lowered cost of transportation, rising affluence and auto ownership, and a persistent desire among households for the quality of life offered by larger houses, more open space, better schools, and other amenities led to a dramatic shift towards the suburbs and away from dense central cities. Partly as the result of this residential suburbanization, and partly as the result of the construction of extensive circumferential as well as radial freeways, the suburban shopping mall became a dominant part of the urban landscape in the past three decades. Suburban shopping malls presaged the creation of suburban office parks during the past two decades, and the decentralization of much of the service industry jobs which had traditionally occupied the central business district. As the highway system has expanded over this period, and auto ownership has continued to rise, the entire shape of metropolitan areas has been redefined from a CBD dominated, dense urban area with a relatively small diameter, to a sprawling mix of land uses of much lower density, with suburban office and industrial parks rivaling the dominance of the CBD, and the spawning of an 'exurban' ring outside of the suburbs.

The impact of highway investments on residential and employment location has been evident over these past several decades, but related questions remain less clear. The loss of the primacy of the CBD's, for example, has caused many central cities to consider large investments in heavy radial rail systems to attempt to restore vitality to these declining urban centers. It remains to be seen, however, to what extent such investments will be able to counteract the trend set in place through several decades if highway investments, and the gradual shift in consumer preferences and attitudes over time.

Models of residential and employment location have received extensive use in most large urban areas as an input into the transportation planning process. Typically, these are applied land use models with little behavioral or policy sensitivity. Some efforts have been made to integrate transportation models with land use models, such as Putman's (1983) ITLUP model system, and Anas's (1982) CATLAS model. Most metropolitan transportation planning agencies, however, prepare a land use forecast without specific sensitivity to a particular transportation system assumption, and subsequently conduct alternatives analysis on transportation investments given the exogenous population and employment distribution forecast.

A more effective approach for analyzing public investments in highways, high occupancy vehicle lanes, rail systems, and bus systems, would be to integrate the land use and travel demand models with the land use models. This would allow for the assessment of both the land use impacts of particular transport investments and the travel demand generated by a given distribution of residences and workplaces.

With the exception of the bidirectional nature of the influence of transportation policies on residential and workplace choices, the nature of these influences seems fairly clear, and can be summarized by one issue: accessibility.

The role of accessibility in the household's choice of residence and workplace location necessitates the analysis of these two decisions with reference to each other. Residence locations are not chosen in a vacuum; they are chosen, among other factors, with reference to the workplace location. This requirement becomes absolute as distances of potential residence locations from a household's workplace location become large enough to encounter the household's time or budget constraint. Although it is clear enough that the choice of residence and workplace locations are related decisions, for individual workers the nature and sequence of those decisions becomes less clear.

Urban labor and housing markets

The implications of households' choices of residence and workplace location, travel mode, and tenure for urban labor and housing markets are difficult to disentangle, and have been a source of controversy for some time. Two decades ago, Kain (1968) published a seminal paper on what has come to be known as the spatial mismatch hypothesis, initiating a policy debate which today still remains divisive. Kain's focus was on the deleterious effects which housing segregation and suburbanizing employment had on the employment prospects of ghetto-bound blacks. Since the line of policy research stimulated by the debate surrounding the spatial mismatch hypothesis is central to the issues of transportation, urban labor and housing markets, and discrimination, and represent the limitations of past research efforts to effectively separate these issues, it will be reviewed in some detail in this section.

Kain's study was a deceptively simple analysis of the ghettoes in Detroit and Chicago, using data on place of work and place of residence from the home interview survey of the Chicago Area Transportation Study of 1956 and the Detroit Area Traffic Study of 1952. He evaluated three related hypotheses: "that racial segregation in the housing market (1) affects the distribution of Negro employment, and (2) reduces Negro job opportunities, and that (3) postwar suburbanization of employment has seriously aggravated the problem." To test the hypothesis, Kain estimated a series of multiple regression models in which the dependent variable was the percentage of the total employment in each of 98 work zones in Chicago and Detroit who were black (W).

Two independent variables were used in Kain's analysis. The first is the percentage of the population within each work zone who are black. This variable was intended to act as a proxy for the propensity of employers to discriminate for or against nonwhite workers on the basis of the real or imagined attitudes of the residential population in the area toward the employment of blacks. The second independent variable is distance of the workplace zone from the ghetto.

Kain simulated the effect of dispersing the ghetto by replacing the percentage black variable for each zone with the metropolitan average percentage black, and setting the distance to the ghetto variable to zero. The results, Kain argued, showed that housing segregation cost Chicago blacks between 22,000 and 24,000 jobs, and cost Detroit blacks between 3,000 and 9,000 jobs. These results were further used by Kain and others to argue that efforts to spur economic development in the ghetto are counterproductive, since the spatial concentration and lack of accessibility of the ghetto are the key elements limiting the employment opportunities of blacks. Instead, Kain argued, better enforcement of the open housing laws, subsidized construction of low cost housing in the suburbs, or housing subsidies directly to the poor would be more productive strategies.

Shortly after Kain's (1968) findings were published, the Watts riots shook the city of Los Angeles and the nation. Kain's paper was cited by the McCone Commission, the Kerner Commission, and the Urban Mass Transportation Administration, all of which agreed with the proposition that the lack of access to suburban jobs was one of the significant causes of the high unemployment which ultimately led to the Watts riots. The policy debate had begun.

Subsequent researchers questioned the validity of Kain's methods as well as his conclusions. Mooney (1969) performed regressions on the poorest census tracts of 25 SMSAs using 1960 census data to test the Kain hypothesis that restrictions on the residential choice of blacks reduced their employment. Mooney concluded from his analysis that the tightness of the metropolitan labor market was the most significant variable affecting black employment levels, and that the lack of accessibility of central city blacks to the suburban area was relatively small. Kain (1975) responded to Mooney's analysis by criticizing in particular the measure of accessibility, which was implied by ratios of central city employment to total metropolitan employment, and by the ratio of nonwhite males who work outside the central city and live in the central city to the total number of nonwhite males who live in the central city and work in the SMSA. Much of the subsequent research either in support of or against the Kain hypothesis dealt with the specification issue, and particularly with the specification of the influence of accessibility.

Harrison (1974) provided the next major critique, using data on white and nonwhite males residing in central city poverty tracts, central city nonpoverty tracts, and suburban tracts in 12 SMSAs. By analyzing frequency distributions of weekly earnings, employment, occupation, education, and training program participation, Harrison found that central city nonwhites in nonpoverty tracts had higher earnings than either nonwhites in central city poverty tracts or in suburban areas. White earnings, on the other hand, were highest in suburban areas, lower in central city nonpoverty areas, and lowest in central city poverty areas. He also found that the marginal returns to schooling were substantial for whites, regardless of their location, but nonwhites received almost no reductions in unemployment by staying in school, regardless of their location. Harrison's most significant argument was that central city employment was actually growing, and that enough low and semi-skilled jobs were being created in the central city to eliminate all ghetto unemployment, if the jobs had gone to ghetto residents. Instead, the jobs were being taken predominantly by suburban residents.

Kain's (1975) response to these arguments emphasized the fact that Harrison used data on nonwhites rather than specifically on blacks, which might confuse the analysis since Harrison's sample of 12 SMSAs included four with significant proportions of nonwhites which were not black (Houston, Los Angeles, New York, and San Francisco). Kain also criticized Harrison's pooling of the data for the 12 SMSAs, which he claimed eliminated the potential for separating the issues of housing and accessibility.

One of the more damaging critiques of the Kain hypothesis was one by Offner and Saks (1971). This critique focused on Kain's model specification, which they claimed was overly sensitive to alternative specifications. By repeating Kain's analysis on the same data, but with the percentage of black residents entered into the model as a squared term rather than a simple term, Offner and Saks were able to produce opposite results from Kain's simulation.

The last critique of this hypothesis to be noted here is one by Ellwood (1978), which analyzed two ghettoes in Chicago with very different proximities to employment centers. Ellwood found that black residents of both ghettoes fared worse than the white residents of either in their employment rates, leading him to conclude that accessibility was not a significant detriment to the employment level of ghetto blacks.

The debate on the true impact of residential segregation and lack of accessibility to suburban employment for ghetto blacks has not been fully resolved even after two decades, nor has the resulting policy debate as to whether to invest in economic development in the ghetto, provide public transportation from the ghetto to suburban employment centers, or concentrate on decentralizing the ghettoes through housing vouchers and other means. Much of the reason for the stalemate on these debates appears to be due to inadequacies in the methods and data employed in these analyses, and in particular, the inability of these analyses to effectively measure and isolate the role of accessibility.

4 The region, the data, and the model

The development of the present model of worker's choices of residence location, workplace location, and housing tenure extends a similar model developed by Anas (1982) for the Chicago area called CATLAS. In the CATLAS model, Anas predicted mode choice and residential location given workplace locations using a nested logit model. Two models were estimated, one for CBD workers, and one for all non-CBD workers. Anas used aggregate data from three sets of tabulations from the 1970 census. The first set of tabulations describes the employment within each zone by industry, occupation, and sex. The second set of tabulations describes the resident population of each zone, its households, and dwellings. The third is a tabulation of work trips by origin (residence zone), destination (workplace zone), and mode of travel.

The CATLAS model laid a very solid foundation for further research by formulating a nested logit model of residence location and mode choice which was well grounded in random utility theory, and used readily available aggregate data rather than disaggregate data. Anas (1982) demonstrated several useful findings:

> Choice models estimated from small area data can be at least as meaningful, useful, and transferable as equivalent choice models estimated from disaggregate data.
>
> Comparison of the elasticities for rent, travel cost, and travel time of our aggregate models to the same elasticities of disaggregate models estimated by others shows that there is no discernible persistent difference. Differences among the elasticities of our estimated models can be substantial and due to specification decisions, yet the ranges of our elasticities compare extremely well with the ranges of the estimated elasticities generated from disaggregate models.
>
> Our study confirms that IID probit and multinomial logit models yield virtually identical results.

Although both nested and nonnested logit demand models perform quite well in elasticities and in aggregate prediction, the nested logit models appear to be substantially more robust in prediction and to yield coefficients that are more stable in the face of specification changes.

Important inclusion-exclusion relationships among explanatory attributes govern the specification of location-mode choice models. Attributes measuring or proxying public services, neighborhood quality, and location are important in obtaining acceptable estimates of the coefficients of rent, travel cost, and travel time.

Two important limitations of the CATLAS model due to the nature of the data available were identified by Anas (1982). The first is the restriction of having to pool homeowners and renters. Were data on tenure choices available, the models could be extended to represent the interaction of travel mode, residential location, and housing tenure choices, while at the same time treating rentals and housing prices as separate attributes. The second limitation is the lack of detail on the choices of households and their members.

The present study overcomes the limitations identified by Anas by developing a special tabulation of the 1980 Census Urban Transportation Planning Package (UTPP), which provides a rich level of detail on individual workers, their household characteristics, and their choices of residence location, workplace location, and housing tenure. In a similar vein to the model extensions envisioned by Anas to a nested logit model of travel mode, residential location, and housing tenure, we will develop and estimate a multidimensional choice model of workplace, residence, and housing tenure. Some of the limitations identified by Anas in his earlier work can be overcome in this study by using more detailed data. A second extension of prior models is the separate estimation of the model by race, in order to evaluate the degree to which the structure of choices varies by race. A third extension of prior research is an analysis of the structure of and relationship between the three dimensions of choice under examination: residence location, housing tenure, and workplace location by testing alternative nested logit model specifications.

Geographic scope

The area used in this analysis is two county core of the Dallas-Fort Worth SMSA. The selection of Dallas-Fort Worth as a study area should provide useful insights into patterns of residential and workplace choice for several reasons. The metropolitan area is very young, having experienced more than half of its population growth within the past two decades. As a young area, its form has been shaped predominantly by massive public investments in the highway system. In addition, the rapid growth of the region has accelerated the geographic sorting out of persons of different race, ethnicity, age, household type, and socioeconomic status. The region has experienced over the past two decades very rapid turnover of population, and almost overnight creation of new neighborhoods, office and industrial parks, and transportation systems by aggressive developer and public investment in response to the region's economic boom. As a result, a current snapshot of the geographic patterning of the region's population and jobs should provide more insight into the underlying choices made by individuals and households than do older cities which have lower rates of population turnover and larger proportions of relatively older, fixed infrastructure.

The geographic level of analysis used in this study is the census tract, of which there are 650 in the Dallas-Fort Worth SMSA. Over 80 percent of the population, and over 95 percent of the employment in the SMSA was located within the two central counties of Dallas and Tarrant in 1980. The geographic scope of this study is confined to this two county metropolitan area in order to provide greater geographic resolution within the metropolitan core, and to avoid problems of incomplete data in outlying counties.

Data

As noted earlier, prior studies of the residential and workplace locational preferences of workers have faced limitations in the data available for such analysis, either in terms of a lack of geographic detail, or the demographic and socioeconomic characteristics of the chooser, or having data with which to examine the relationships between different types of choices, such as residential location, workplace location, and housing tenure. The data used in this study are derived from a special tabulation the 1980 Census Journey to Work internal Microdata, and provides a large sample of workers with the census tract location of both residence and workplace, and substantial demographic and socioeconomic characteristics of the workers. The nature of the data should support an unprecedented level of detail in the analysis of the household choice dimensions under investigation here. A description of both the original data and the special tabulation are provided in the following sections.

The urban transportation planning package

The data used in this study originate from a data file prepared by the Census Bureau for the 1980 Urban Transportation Planning Package (UTPP). The data in the UTPP are based on the 1980 census sample of housing units which received the long-form questionnaire on April 1, 1980. While the short-form census questionnaire was intended to be a 100 percent sample of housing units, the supplementary long-form questionnaire was completed for approximately one in every six housing units, except in counties, places, or minor civil divisions with fewer than 2500 persons (based on precensus estimates), which had a one in two sample rate. The resulting nationwide average sample rate was approximately 19 percent of all housing units.

To provide data which would be useful for transportation planning activities, a subsample of approximately half of the census long-form questionnaire sample was prepared in which the workplace, travel time to work, and migration data items were coded. This procedure generated a microdata (one person per record) file with detailed demographic and socioeconomic characteristics of the worker, as well as the census tract location of both residence and workplace. The procedure for the selection of this subsample is summarized in the Technical Documentation for Summary Tape, U.S Census Bureau (1983):

> In order to reduce the cost of processing, a scheme was designed, while the sample questionnaires were being processed, to select a sample of questionnaires on which the place of work, travel time to work, and migration data items would be coded. The sample questionnaires were processed by work units consisting of 1980 census EDs. In work units (EDs) where the place of work, travel time to work, and migration data items had not yet been coded, every other sample questionnaire within the work unit was selected for these coding operations. In work units where the place of work, travel time to work, and migration data items already had been coded, all sample questionnaires were included in the tabulation.

The sample data were adjusted to approximate a 100 percent sample using an iterative ratio estimation procedure which resulted in the assignment of a weight to each sample person or housing unit record. For a detailed description of this estimation procedure, see Fulton (1983). As a byproduct of the estimation procedure, it should be noted that the estimates from the sample are, for the most part, consistent with complete-count figures for the population and housing unit records used in the estimation procedure.

As a final step before release of the data to metropolitan planning agencies which contracted for these services, the data were processed into a series of tabulations which had been previously submitted to the Census Bureau by an ad hoc committee representing the Transportation Research Board's Committee on Transportation Information Systems and Data Requirements. The data in the form it was released for the UTPP contained a series of tables of worker characteristics by residence zone, tables of worker characteristics by workplace zone, and selected tables of workers by residence zone and by workplace zone, which provided a trip matrix. The only data associated with the residence zone by workplace zone tables, however, were the number of workers by means of transportation, and the associated travel times. Although this data was relatively useful, it did not provide a journey to work trip matrix separately for workers by demographic and socioeconomic category, which would make the data much more useful for the analysis of household choices of residence location, workplace location, and housing tenure.

Suppression

The data from which the UTPP tabulations were prepared includes a microdata file with one worker per record, and an extensive list of individual and household demographic and socioeconomic characteristics, as well as the residence zone and workplace census tract geocodes. While this data would be much more valuable for the purposes of studies of residential location and workplace location, the Census Bureau does not release the data in microdata form because of its suppression requirements for protecting the confidentiality of respondents. In microdata form, geocodes of residence place must include at least 100,000 persons in order to be released by the Census Bureau. For most intra-metropolitan analyses, particularly where accessibility is a central research question, zones of 100,000 or more persons are much too large to be useful, rendering access to these data in microdata form relatively useless.

Different suppression criteria apply to census tabulations, however. Although tabular, or aggregate, data is generally less desirable than microdata due to within cell variation, It is possible to construct a tabulation of these microdata which all but eliminate the within cell variance by producing an extremely fine cross-classification of characteristics. The relevant suppression criteria for such tabulations are summarized below from the technical documentation:

1. No Suppression: The counts which are not subject to suppression are total population, total housing units, year-round housing units, vacant year-round housing units, count of persons and households for each race or Spanish origin group.

2. Primary Suppression: Characteristics of persons other than race or Spanish origin are shown only if there are 30 or more persons residing in the geographic area. Characteristics of year-round housing units are suppressed only if there are fewer than 10 year-round housing units within the geographic area, regardless of the number of persons. Characteristics of families, households, or housing units are shown if there are at least 10 housing units within the geographic area.

Additional suppression criteria apply if the tabulation is cross-classified by race or Spanish origin. This level requires that at least 30 persons or 10 households are present for each race or Spanish origin group in order to avoid suppression.

3   Complementary Suppression: In some cases data are suppressed to prevent the derivation of suppressed data by subtraction.

Special tabulation

In order to derive a data file for this study with the maximum relevant detail on the demographic and socioeconomic characteristics of workers, as well as their residence and workplace locations and commuting times, a special request was made to the Journey to Work and Migration Division of the Census Bureau. The Census Bureau agreed to produce a special tabulation of the FEMA 1980 Census Worker Subfile, which is a microdata file with one worker per record. Three conditions were made. First, the program to process the data and produce the tabulation would be provided to the Census Bureau for internal execution. Second, the tabulation must meet the relevant suppression criteria. And third, the individual records would be weighted by the sample weight to expand the sample to the full population.

The essence of the tabulation program is that worker records cross-classified by 12 socioeconomic and demographic characteristics, as well as by tenure, travel mode to work, census tract of residence, and census tract of work. Means of several additional characteristics were calculated for each of the cells in the cross-classification. It should be noted that producing a cross-classification of 16 simultaneous variables in this manner produces a very sparse matrix, with most cells empty, and many of the cells having only one unweighted record meeting the unique combination of the 16 characteristics. In order to economize on the size of the file, only the non-zero cells of the matrix were written to a file.

Although the Census Journey to Work data contain commuting travel time information, these figures represent the perceived travel time of workers, that is, how they recall the average time they travel to work. In transportation planning studies, more accurate estimates of zone to zone travel time are generally obtained from extensive data collection and transportation network simulation. Tract to tract peak hour travel times for 1980 were obtained for this study from the North Central Texas Council of Governments, the metropolitan planning agency responsible for transportation planning in Dallas-Fort Worth.

The following table summarizes the characteristics on which the tabulation was based:

Table 4.1 Cross-classification characteristics

DESCRIPTION	CATEGORIES
Relationship to Head	Head of Household
	Not Head of Household
Race/Spanish Origin	White-Not Hispanic
	Black-Not Hispanic
	Other-Not Hispanic
	Hispanic
Sex	Male
	Female
Household Type	Husband/Wife Family
	Male Householder Family
	Female Householder Family
	Nonfamily Householder
Tenure	Rent
	Own
Means of Transportation	Auto or Truck
	Public Transportation
Auto/Truck Ownership	0 Autos/Trucks
	1
	2
	3 or More
Family Income	Less than $10,000
	$10,000 - $19,999
	$20,000 - $29,999
	$30,000 - $39,999
	$40,000 - $49,999
	$50,000 - $59,999
	$60,000 - $69,999
	$70,000 - $79,999
	$80,000 - $89,999
	$90,000 - $99,999
	$100,000 or More

Table 4.1 Continued

DESCRIPTION	CATEGORIES
Age Group	Less than 20
	20 - 29
	30 - 39
	40 - 49
	50 - 59
	60 or More
Number of Workers in Household	1
	2
	3
	4 or More
Year Structure Built	1979 or 1980
	1975 to 1978
	1970 to 1974
	1960 to 1969
	1950 to 1959
	1940 to 1949
	1939 or earlier
Class of Worker	Employee of private business
	Federal government employee
	State government employee
	Local government employee
	Self employed - not incorporated
	Self employed - incorporated
	Work without pay in family business
Industry of Worker	3 Digit Census Industry Code
Occupation of Worker	3 Digit Census Occupation Code
Census Tract	650 Census Tracts (SMSA)
Census Tract of Work	650 Census Tracts (SMSA)

Mean characteristics

In addition to these variables included in the cross-classification list, for which there will be zero within-cell variance, several additional variables were used to calculate means for each cell of the cross-classification identified above. The variables for which cell means were calculated are the following:

Table 4.2 Characteristics for which means were calculated

DESCRIPTION
Age of worker in years
Family income
Years of school completed
Hours worked last week
Weeks looking for work in 1979
Usual Hours worked per week in 1979
One way travel time to work in minutes (to 99)
Social Security income in 1979 (in hundreds)
Wages or salary in 1979 (in hundreds)
Public Assistance income in 1979 (in hundreds)
Nonfarm, self-employment income in 1979 (in hundreds)
All other income in 1979 (in hundreds)
Farm, self-employment income in 1979 (in hundreds)
Property income in 1979 (in hundreds)

Data restrictions

In order to most effectively analyze the choices of residence location, workplace location, and housing tenure, the sample used in model estimation was restricted to include workers employed full time in 1979, who lived and worked in either Dallas or Tarrant County, and who were household heads in married couple families in which only one of the couple worked in 1979, or were household heads of single parent households, or were members of non-family households. The reason for this restriction in the initial analysis is that within family households in which both husband and wife work it is likely that the locational calculus of the household is much more complicated than that of a household with only one wage earner. The case of multiple-worker households will be the subject of a separate study.

Rather than balancing a residential location to fit the accessibility needs of two earners to separate workplace locations, single worker households would presumably take into consideration the workplace location of only the household head in choosing their residence location, along with the remaining array of residential location characteristics to be considered. Workers in non-family households could be expected to choose their residential location more independently of other household members than would family households, although this generalization might be less valid for unmarried couples living together.

Two census tracts of residence were identified by the Census Bureau as subject to suppression (31.02 and 137.05). These two census tracts are both high density commercial areas, and were recoded to the tract number of an adjacent tract (22.02 and 136.01, respectively) prior to executing the tabulation, in order to avoid any suppression in the final data file.

Workers were restricted to include only those who owned an vehicle, and did not rely on transit to commute to work. While this eliminates the poorest segment of the population, often known as 'transit captives' from the sample, they represent less than two percent of the total workers, and would clearly have a different decisionmaking structure for the choice of residence, workplace, and housing tenure than the balance of the population who are more mobile. In particular, their choices of residence, and perhaps workplace as well, are extremely constrained by the availability of transit service. The locational choices of this group was therefore determined to warrant further investigation in a separate analysis.

It should be noted that the identification of workers is based on the response of individuals to the census household survey questionnaire, and not on a business establishment based reporting scheme. The nature of the responses, therefore, represents only the primary job of each worker, and does not include any other secondary jobs the worker may hold.

Model specification

In developing and estimating models of locational choice which incorporate significant information about the demographic and socioeconomic characteristics of both the chooser and the choice, a determination must be made regarding the degree to which the data should be stratified for separate model estimation, or pooled with interaction terms added to the models. Several stratification approaches were evaluated for this study, including various combinations of race, age, income, housing tenure, household type, and education. The models developed and estimated here reflect a stratification of the population only by race, with terms added to the models to account for hypothesized interactions.

The population groups with adequate representation in the sample for model estimation were Blacks, Whites (non-Hispanic), and Hispanics. This model estimation strategy assumes that the underlying preferences are the same between persons of the same racial or ethnic group, except as measured by the interaction terms included in the model.

The model derivation and specification will be presented for the choice of workplace location, housing tenure, and residential location. Since the choice set under investigation contains three distinct choice dimensions, the models specified and tested include both joint multinomial logit and nested logit structures. Analysis of these alternative specifications should resolve any potential concern regarding biases arising from violations of the Independence of Irrelevant Alternatives (IIA) property.

Characteristics of residential locations

A large body of literature exists on the factors which influence the perception of the desirability of alternative residential locations. Workplace accessibility has been cited by Quigley (1976), Harrison and MacDonald (1974), and many others as one of the most significant factors influencing housing values. Other analysts, such as Ridker (1967), and Freeman (1979), have found significant effects on housing values from environmental variables such as air quality. Perhaps the largest and most diverse set of influences on residential desirability are neighborhood characteristics. This broad category of factors includes the socioeconomic mix of a neighborhood, its racial and ethnic composition, the age distribution of the population, crime levels, school quality, and physical amenities or disamenities such as parks, golf courses, or incompatible land uses. Racial mix has been included in housing value studies by Rose-Ackerman (1975), Yinger (1976), and Courant and Yinger (1977). Anderson and Crocker (1972) have included median incomes and crime levels in similar studies on housing value.

One of the difficulties in effectively specifying a model of residential attractiveness is the potential for including independent variables which can be argued to be endogenous. For example, including the median neighborhood income level in a model to predict the location of high income households would clearly provide little analytical insight into the true influences on the desirability of the neighborhood which led to the concentration of high income households there to begin with. In the present study, the stock of housing, and the prices of that housing are taken to be exogenous. Individual households are considered to be price takers. Since the construction of housing and the determination of clearing prices is a market operation, however, resulting from the interaction between households' demand functions for housing and developers' supply functions, many of the exogenous influences on the desirability of residential locations, such as school quality, crime levels, and neighborhood appearance will already have been capitalized into the price of the housing. Housing prices will therefore serve as a proxy for several of these factors for which no data were available for this study.

As Shevky and Bell (1955) and Berry (1977) have shown, consistent with the theory of social ecology, families tend to segregate by three groups of criteria: socioeconomic status, stage of life cycle, and race or ethnicity. Given an exogenous housing supply and price, social ecological theory is incorporated into the model in order to isolate these segregation preferences from issues of accessibility, housing supply, price, and other neighborhood amenities. Estimation of these segregation preferences is accomplished by separately estimating the models by race, and by the inclusion of variables describing the socioeconomic and life cycle characteristics of the workers and of the alternative residential locations.

There are several other residential zone characteristics which can be expected to influence the desirability of residential locations, and for which data are available. The age of the housing stock may affect its desirability by representing amenities correlated with the age of the unit and of the neighborhood. Similarly, the residential density of a zone and the proportion of the housing in the zone which is single family may influence its desirability.

Workplace accessibility has been discussed as a dominant influence on the desirability of residential locations, and can be incorporated into the model as a function of the one way travel time from home to work. Other accessibility measures may be relevant as well, such as to shopping, or entertainment, and to other amenities. In a monocentric city, these would be expected to be associated with accessibility to the CBD. In the context of a multinucleated urban area such as the Dallas-Fort Worth SMSA, however, more than one such measure would need to be used. Variables measuring proximity to the Dallas CBD and the Fort Worth CBD would help to capture the effects of multinucleated employment dispersion.

Table 4.3 Characteristics of residential locations

VARIABLE	DESCRIPTION
Workplace Access	Average highway travel time to work
Housing Supply	Proportion SMSA housing, by tenure
Housing Price	Average price of housing, by tenure
Housing Size	Average number of bedrooms
Housing Quality	Percent of housing units boarded up
Housing Age	Average age owner occupied housing
Tenure Distribution	Proportion renter occupied dwellings
Population Density	Total Population per acre
Employment Density	Ratio of population to employment
Dallas CBD Access	Travel time to Dallas CBD squared
Fort Worth CBD Access	Travel time to Fort Worth CBD squared
Black	Percent black residents
Hispanic	Percent Hispanic residents
Families w/ Children	Pct Married Couple Family with Children
Nonfamily Households	Percent Nonfamily Households
Age Above 64	Percent of household heads age over 64

Characteristics of workers

The demographic and socioeconomic characteristics of workers enter the model in one of two ways. First, the population is stratified by race, and the model is estimated separately for blacks, whites, and Hispanics. Second, income, age, education, and life cycle status enter into the model through interaction terms with characteristics of residential locations, housing tenure, or workplace location.

Variables are entered into the model for the interaction between income and the following characteristics: housing price, housing size, housing ownership, and racial composition. Housing is considered to be a normal good, leading to expected positive values on the coefficients for the income interaction terms with housing price, size, and ownership. The percentage of the population in a residence zone of black or Hispanic race and ethnicity, however, is expected to be a 'good' or 'bad' depending on the racial group of the chooser, and the degree of prejudice felt by the chooser towards members of each other racial and ethnic group.

It is hypothesized that whites will consider the percentage black population, and to a lesser extent the percentage Hispanic population, as economic bads, and the signs of coefficients on the income interaction with percent black will be negative for whites, and of a larger magnitude than the coefficient for the interaction with percent Hispanic. Blacks are hypothesized to show a positive and significant relationship with percent black, due to an unknown combination of positive clustering with persons of similar tastes and culture, and negative clustering, or discrimination and flight on the part of whites. As recent research has indicated that blacks prefer to live in integrated neighborhoods rather than all black neighborhoods, we would expect the income interaction with percentage black to be negative for blacks. The tendency for friction between minorities at the low end of the economic ladder leads us to expect that the income interaction for blacks with the percent Hispanic will be negative. Hispanics, for the same reason, are expected to show a negative income interaction with percent black. Hispanics are also expected to show a positive interaction with percent Hispanic, but a negative income interaction with percent Hispanic, reflecting a tendency to leave the 'barrio', and assimilate into white areas as income rises.

Table 4.4 Characteristics of workers

VARIABLE	DESCRIPTION
Income	Family Income
Age	Age of worker
Family Status	Family or non-family household
Over 64	Head of Household over 64

Characteristics of workplaces

The workplace choice dimension of the model has a simple structure, with jobs stratified by skill or educational level into four categories:

1 Unskilled: Less than four years of high school completed,

2 Low Skilled: High school completed,

3 Skilled: One to four years of college completed, or

4 High Skilled: More than four years of college completed.

Given an exogenous spatial distribution of firms, and therefore jobs, it is hypothesized that the probability of a worker choosing a workplace is positively related to the number of jobs of the same skill level as the worker, and positively associated with the wage level offered for those jobs. A series of variables is included in the model to test these simple hypotheses.

In order to test the attractiveness to workers of centralized versus dispersed workplaces, variables are included in the model for the travel time from the workplace from the central business districts of Dallas and Fort Worth. It is hypothesized that the coefficients on these terms will reveal a stronger tendency for whites to choose dispersed workplaces than that for Hispanics and blacks, as a result of more suburban residential choices.

A final set of variables is included in the workplace choice dimension of the model to test the sensitivity of workplace choice to the racial mix of the workplace. The racial mix of the workplace here refers to daytime population at the place of work, stratified by skill level, as opposed to the residential mix included in the residential location choice dimension of the model. It is hypothesized that there may exist significant workplace racial segregation, and that this is more prominent for blacks than for Hispanics.

Table 4.5 Characteristics of workplaces

VARIABLE	DESCRIPTION
Employment Share	Share of regional employment, by skill level
Average Hourly Wage	Average hourly wage, by skill level
Dallas CBD Access	Average travel time to the Dallas CBD
Fort Worth CBD Access	Average travel time to the Fort Worth CBD
Percent Black	Percent black workers, by skill level
Percent Hispanic	Percent Hispanic workers, by skill level

Sources of bias

Although maximum likelihood estimation of these choice models provides asymptotically consistent coefficients, these estimates and the corresponding choice probabilities may be biased by the model specification, aggregation, sampling, segmentation, and other assumptions. Anas (1982) has identified ten potential sources of bias:

1. Specification of the choice model type such as logit, generalized extreme value, and probit;
2. Specification of the form of the choice model's objective function (e.g. utility or profit function) such as linear, loglinear, and generalized constant elasticity of substitution;
3. Specification of the explanatory variables or attributes to be included in the choice model;
4. A precise definition of the choice alternatives;
5. Specification of the assumptions or processes by which the choice set of each chooser is determined (e.g. the list of the choice alternatives to be entered into the choice set of each chooser);
6. Population segmentation or grouping of choosers into distinct categories within which a single and distinct choice model or utility function is sufficient to describe the dispersion of preferences and choices;

7 Aggregation of the choice alternatives into groups (aggregation units) and commensurate aggregation of the attributes (explanatory variables) within each aggregation unit;
8 Sampling of the choosers within each population segment and sampling of the choice alternatives within each chooser's choice set to form an estimation sample;
9 Measurement method used in determining the values of the explanatory variables for each choice alternative and each chooser in the data;
10 Estimation method applied to obtain estimates of the choice model's coefficients.

Joint choice specification

We begin the model derivation by considering three choice sets, W, T, and R, representing workplace, tenure, and residence locations, with w, t, and r elements in the choice sets, respectively. The full choice set then becomes the Cartesian product of these choice sets, or, if they are the infeasible alternatives for individual n, then the full multidimensional choice set becomes

$$C_n = w \times t \times r - C^*_n \qquad 4.1$$

As Ben-Akiva and Lerman (1987) show, there are significant differences between the multinomial choice model in which all the alternatives are within one choice dimension (such as residence location), and the model of multidimensional choice. These differences are based on the fact that some of the alternatives in the full multidimensional choice set share common observed or unobserved attributes. In the current model, for example, some of the elements in the combined choice set share a common residence location, others share a common tenure, and others share a common workplace. If the elements of the choice set share only observed attributes across the choice dimensions, then a joint logit model structure is specified. If, on the other hand, elements of the choice set share both observed and unobserved attributes across the choice dimensions, then a nested logit model is specified. Tests of the appropriateness of the model specification will be discussed in a later section. In this section we will develop the joint logit model under the assumption that the elements of the choice set share only observed attributes between choice dimensions.

The utility function of a worker choosing a workplace location, housing tenure, and residential location can be partitioned into systematic and random components, expressed as

$$\mathbf{U}_{wtr} = \tilde{V}_w + \tilde{V}_t + \tilde{V}_r + \tilde{V}_{wt} + \tilde{V}_{tr} + \tilde{V}_{wr} + \tilde{V}_{wtr} + \tilde{\varepsilon}_{wtr},$$
$$\forall (w,t,r) \in C_n \qquad 4.2$$

where

U_{wtr} is the total utility of workplace (zone) w, housing tenure t, and residence location r.

$\tilde{V}_w$ is the systematic component of the utility of workplace alternative w,

$\tilde{V}_t$ is the systematic component of utility of tenure choice t,

$\tilde{V}_r$ is the systematic component of utility of residence location r,

$\tilde{V}_{wt}$ is the systematic component of utility specific to the combination (w,t),

$\tilde{V}_{tr}$ is the systematic component of utility specific to the combination (t,r),

$\tilde{V}_{wr}$ is the systematic component of utility specific to the combination (w,r),

$\tilde{V}_{wtr}$ is the systematic component of utility specific to the combination (w,t,r), and

ε_{wtr} is the random component of the utility of alternative (w,t,r).

The assumption of independently and identically Gumbel distributed random terms (with the scale parameter normalized to 1) for each alternative allows the use of the multinomial logit model for the joint choice of workplace, tenure, and residence location. This joint logit model can be stated as

$$\mathbf{P}(w,t,r) = \frac{e^{\mu\left(\tilde{V}_w + \tilde{V}_t + \tilde{V}_r + \tilde{V}_{wt} + \tilde{V}_{tr} + \tilde{V}_{wr} + \tilde{V}_{wtr}\right)}}{\sum_{(r',t',w') \in C_n} e^{\mu\left(\tilde{V}_{w'} + \tilde{V}_{t'} + \tilde{V}_{r'} + \tilde{V}_{w't'} + \tilde{V}_{t'r'} + \tilde{V}_{w'r'} + \tilde{V}_{w't'r'}\right)}} \qquad 4.3$$

where μ is a positive scale parameter. In the multinomial logit model, as in the binary logit model, this scale parameter is assumed to equal 1, which expresses the assumption that the disturbances are homoskedastic (Ben-Akiva and Lerman, 1987).

The structure of the joint logit is a simple multinomial logit specification, with all the choices on one level, as opposed to the hierarchical specification of a nested logit model. This structure is shown in figure 4.1 for the three dimensional model of the choice of workplace, tenure, and residential location.

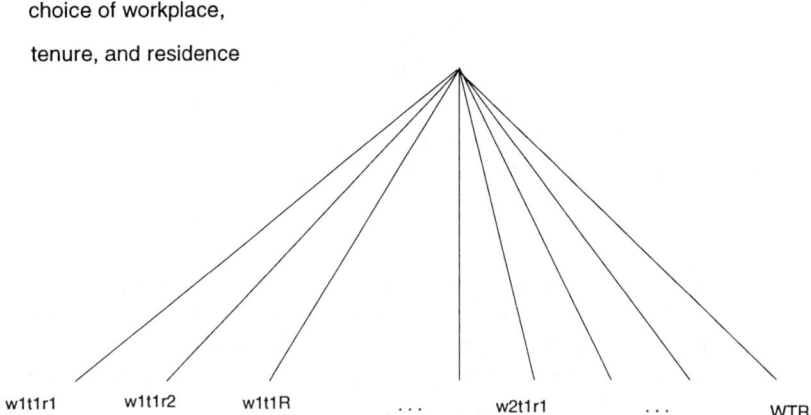

Figure 4.1 The joint logit specification

Sequential choice specification

In the more general case where the scale parameter is not restricted to a value of one, we derive the nested logit model. Using the same choice set as in the previous section, and assuming that elements share both observed and unobserved attributes across choice dimensions, we can rewrite the utility expression as

$$U_{wtr} = \tilde{V}_w + \tilde{V}_t + \tilde{V}_r + \tilde{V}_{wt} + \tilde{V}_{tr} + \tilde{V}_{wr} + \tilde{V}_{wtr}$$
$$+ \tilde{\varepsilon}_w + \tilde{\varepsilon}_t + \tilde{\varepsilon}_r + \tilde{\varepsilon}_{wt} + \tilde{\varepsilon}_{tr} + \tilde{\varepsilon}_{wr} + \tilde{\varepsilon}_{wtr}, \quad \forall (w,t,r) \in C_n \qquad 4.4$$

where

$\tilde{\varepsilon}_w$ is the unobserved component of the total utility attributable to the workplace w,

$\tilde{\varepsilon}_t$ is the unobserved component of the total utility attributable to tenure choice t,

$\tilde{\varepsilon}_r$ is the unobserved component of the total utility attributable to residence location r,

$\tilde{\varepsilon}_{wt}$ is the unobserved component of the total utility attributable to the combination (w,t),

$\tilde{\varepsilon}_{tr}$ is the unobserved component of the total utility attributable to the combination (t,r),

$\tilde{\varepsilon}_{wr}$ is the unobserved component of the total utility attributable to the combination (w,r), and

$\tilde{\varepsilon}_{wtr}$ is the unobserved component of the total utility attributable to the combination of (w,t,r).

The significance of allowing for disturbance terms specific to choice dimensions is that the utilities of the elements of the corresponding multidimensional choice set cannot be independent, thus violating one of the key assumptions underlying the multinomial logit model, the independence of irrelevant alternatives (Ben-Akiva and Lerman, 1987).

Of the two approaches to dealing with this problem, multinomial probit and nested logit, the nested logit model is far less computationally burdensome, and is the approach used here.

In a three dimensional choice set, such as workplace, tenure, and residential location, a nested logit model requires that the dimensions be ordered in such a way that the following conditions are satisfied (Ben-Akiva and Lerman, 1987):

1. All components of the total disturbance involve level 1 (of L choice dimensions), but not all the higher levels have zero variance.

2. All disturbance terms are mutually independent.

3. The sum of the disturbance terms at level 1 and those at the next lower level are identically Gumbel distributed.

In terms of the three choice dimensions under consideration in this study, the literature would suggest that the most plausible ordering of these choices would be workplace, then housing tenure, then residence location. Almost all models of residential location, from the monocentric model of Alonso, Mills, and Muth, to the gravity models of Lowry, Garin, Wilson, and Putman, treat employment location as exogenous to residential location. Workplace is treated as the marginal choice, with residential location the conditional choice.

The choice of housing tenure is hypothesized to be marginal to residential location, and conditioned by the workplace choice. This nesting of choices appears to be the most plausible initial structuring of the choice dimensions prior to explicitly testing model specification, and will be used to further elaborate the model.

The three choice dimensions can be viewed as a hierarchy of decisions, with a worker choosing first his or her preferred workplace, then choosing whether to rent or buy a home given the workplace choice, income, and other factors, and then choosing a residential location, given the choices of workplace and housing tenure already made. Figures 4.2 and 4.3 depict the choice hierarchy as a tree structure for a two level and a three level nested logit model of the choice of workplace, tenure, and residential location:

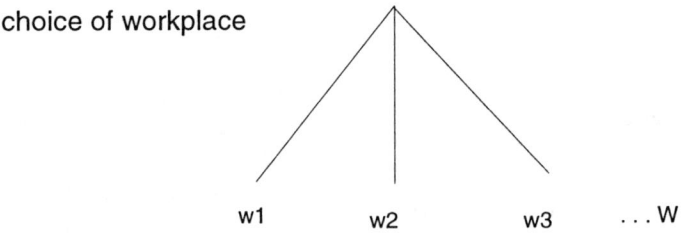

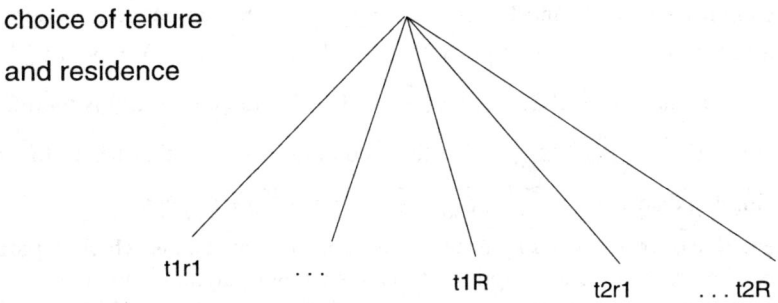

Figure 4.2 2-Level nested logit specification

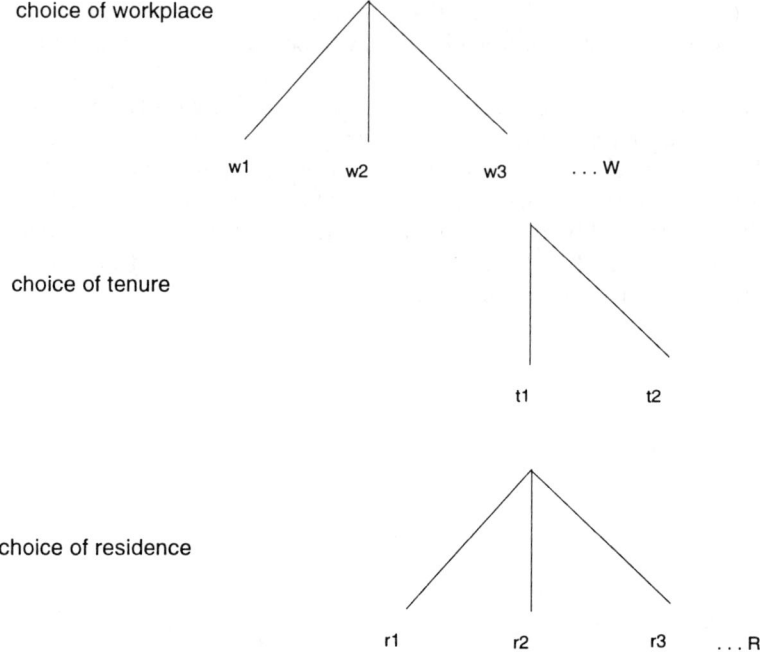

Figure 4. 3   3-Level nested logit specification

Following the notation of Ben-Akiva and Lerman (1987), given the ordering of these choices as W, T, and R, representing workplace, tenure, and residential location, condition 1 above implies that for level 1, $\text{var}(\tilde{\varepsilon}_r) = \text{var}(\tilde{\varepsilon}_{tr}) = \text{var}(\tilde{\varepsilon}_{wr}) = 0$; and for level 2, that $\text{var}(\tilde{\varepsilon}_t) = 0$. The random utility is therefore assumed to be $\tilde{\varepsilon}_w + \tilde{\varepsilon}_{tr} + \tilde{\varepsilon}_{wtr}$. The third condition implies that the following are all Gumbel distributed: $\tilde{\varepsilon}_{wtr}$, $\tilde{\varepsilon}_{wt} + \tilde{\varepsilon}_{wtr}$, and $\tilde{\varepsilon}_w + \tilde{\varepsilon}_{wt} + \tilde{\varepsilon}_{wtr}$.

If there does not exist a sequence of the choice dimensions which satisfies these conditions, then the assumption of the nested logit model is violated.

Given the preceding assumptions, the nested logit choice probability can be expressed as the product of marginal and conditional choice probabilities, each of which is itself a logit model:

$$\mathbf{P}_n(wtr) = P_n(r|wt) P_n(t|w) P_n(w), \qquad 4.5$$

where,

$$\mathbf{P}_n(r|wt) = \frac{e^{(\tilde{V}_r + \tilde{V}_{tr} + \tilde{V}_{wr} + \tilde{V}_{wtr})\mu^r}}{\sum_{r' \in R_{nwt}} e^{(\tilde{V}_{r'} + \tilde{V}_{tr'} + \tilde{V}_{wr'} + \tilde{V}_{wtr'})\mu^r}} \qquad 4.6$$

$$\mathbf{P}_n(t|w) = \frac{e^{(\tilde{V}_t + \tilde{V}_{wt} + V'_{wt})\mu^t}}{\sum_{t' \in T_{nt}} e^{(\tilde{V}_{t'} + \tilde{V}_{wt'} + V'_{wt'})\mu^t}} \qquad 4.7$$

$$\mathbf{P}_n(w) = \frac{e^{(\tilde{V}_w + V'_w)\mu^w}}{\sum_{w' \in W_n} e^{(\tilde{V}_{w'} + V'_{w'})\mu^w}}, \qquad 4.8$$

and where

$$\mathbf{V}'_{wt} = \frac{1}{\mu^r} \ln \sum_{r \in R_{nwt}} e^{(\tilde{V}_r + \tilde{V}_{tr} + \tilde{V}_{wr} + \tilde{V}_{wtr})\mu^r}, \qquad 4.9$$

$$\mathbf{V}'_w = \frac{1}{\mu^t} \ln \sum_{t \in T_{nw}} e^{(\tilde{V}_t + \tilde{V}_{wt} + V'_{wt})\mu^t}. \qquad 4.10$$

In order to satisfy the earlier assumptions of the nested logit model, the ratios μ^t/μ^r and μ^w/μ^t must both be positive and less than or equal to 1. This would satisfy the condition that the variances of the random utilities is the smallest at the lowest level of the tree, and cannot decrease from a lower to a higher level:

$$\mu^w \leq \mu^t \leq \mu^r.$$

In the special case in which $\mu^w = \mu^t = \mu^r$, we obtain the joint logit model (Ben-Akiva and Lerman, 1987).

Sampling of alternatives

The independence of irrelevant alternatives property permits the use of a sample of alternatives in specifying a multinomial logit model with a large number of alternatives. McFadden (1978) established a positive conditioning property as a condition for a consistent estimator for the logit model with samples of alternatives, and uses it to prove that maximization of a conditional log likelihood function yields consistent estimates of the unknown parameters under normal regularity assumptions (see also Ben-Akiva and Lerman, 1987, and for applications to destination choice models, Silman, 1980, and Kozel and Swait, 1982).

In a model of multidimensional choice of workplace, tenure, and residence location such as the present model, the number of potential alternatives is the cartesian product of the alternatives in each dimension. With 528 workplace census tracts, 2 tenure choices, and 528 residence census tracts, there are a total of 557,568 possible alternatives, clearly requiring the use of a sampling of alternatives strategy in order to develop a model which is computationally tractable.

Although several sampling methods can be used, including simple random sampling, importance sampling, independent importance sampling, importance sampling with replacement, and stratified importance sampling, we use a simple random sample of two alternatives for the workplace and residence location dimensions of the choice model. This provides a total of 8 alternatives in the choice model, resulting in a tractable model.

Estimation procedure

The nest two sections describe the estimation procedure for the multinomial and the nested logit specifications. It should be noted that two variants of the multinomial logit model are encountered in the literature, and that the nomenclature is not always consistent. Greene (1986) identifies these two implementations as the multinomial logit model, in which the independent variables are principally chararacteristics of the choosers, and the conditional logit, or discrete choice model developed by McFadden (1973), in which the variables represent characteristics of the alternatives. Our model is principally of the latter type, since we are using the characteristics of residences and workplaces to predict the probability of choosing them. It is a mixed model, however, to the extent that we incorporate some characteristics of the chooser through interaction terms. For further discussion, see Greene (1986). For consistency in the narrative, we will continue to use the term multinomial logit to describe the model being estimated.

Multinomial logit

The estimation of the unknown parameters in the multinomial logit model uses a maximum likelihood estimation procedure developed by McFadden (1974). A brief summary of the estimation procedure is presented here, drawing on a more thorough description by Ben-Akiva and Lerman (1987), and using their notation.

Let N denote the sample size, and define $y_{in}=1$ if observation n chose alternative i, 0 otherwise. The likelihood function for a general multinomial choice model is

$$\mathbf{L}^* = \prod_{n=1}^{N} \prod_{i \in C_n} P_n(i)^{y_{in}}, \qquad 4.11$$

where for a linear-in-parameters logit

$$\mathbf{P}_n = \frac{e^{\beta' x_{in}}}{\sum_{j \in C_n} e^{\beta' x_{jn}}}. \qquad 4.12$$

Taking the logarithm of the likelihood function, we maximize

$$\mathbf{L} = \sum_{n=1}^{N} \sum_{i \in C_n} y_{in}\left(\beta' x_{in} - \ln \sum_{j \in C_n} e^{\beta' x_{jn}}\right). \qquad 4.13$$

The necessary first order conditions are obtained by setting the first derivatives of with respect to the coefficients equal to zero:

$$\frac{\partial \mathbf{L}}{\partial \hat{\beta}_k} = \sum_{n=1}^{N} \sum_{i \in C_n} y_{in}\left(x_{ink} - \frac{\sum_{j \in C_n} e^{\beta' x_{jn}} x_{jnk}}{\sum_{j \in C_n} e^{\beta' x_{jn}}}\right) = 0, \text{ for k=1, ..., K.} \quad 4.14$$

Or,

$$\sum_{n=1}^{N} \sum_{i \in C_n} [y_{in} - P_n(i)] x_{ink} = 0, \text{ for k=1, ..., K.} \qquad 4.15$$

McFadden (1974) has shown that if a solution to this equation exists, it is unique, under relatively weak conditions. Ben-Akiva and Lerman (1987) demonstrate that under general conditions, maximum likelihood estimates are consistent, asymptotically efficient, and asymptotically normal.

The software used to estimate the models for this study is LIMDEP, developed by Greene (1986). The maximum likelihood procedure used to estimate the unknown parameters in the multinomial logit models (called discrete choice models by Greene) is Newton's method, and the variance matrix for the coefficients is estimated with the second derivatives of the log-likelihood:

$$\frac{\partial^2 L}{\partial \hat{\beta}_k \partial \hat{\beta}_l} = -\sum_{n=1}^{N} \sum_{i \in C_n} P_n(i) \left[x_{ink} - \sum_{j \in C_n} x_{jnk} P_n(j) \right] \cdot \left[x_{inl} - \sum_{j \in C_n} x_{jnl} P_n(j) \right]. \quad 4.16$$

Nested logit

As noted earlier, under the circumstances that the scale factors () in the utility expression of a multidimensional choice model equal one, the model reduces to a joint logit model. In this case, the estimation procedures described in the previous section apply directly. In the more general case where these scale parameters are not restricted to a value of one, however, the nested logit model is the correct specification, and changes are necessary in the estimation approach.

In the three dimensional choice model of workplace, tenure, and residential location, the likelihood function is

$$L^* = \prod_{n=1}^{N} \prod_{(r,t,w) \in C_n} \left[P_n(w,t,r) \right]^{y_{wtrn}} \quad 4.17$$

$$= \prod_{n=1}^{N} \prod_{(r,t,w) \in C_n} \left[P_n(r|wt) P_n(t|w) P_n(w) \right]^{y_{wtrn}}, \quad 4.18$$

where $y_{wtrn} = 1$ if observation n chose alternative $(w,t,r) \in C_n$, 0 otherwise.

Maximization of this likelihood function yields consistent and asymptotically efficient estimated of the parameters, and is the most direct approach to estimating the unknown parameters, but it is cumbersome computationally, and few of the econometric estimating packages support this approach. An alternative approach to estimating the parameters in a nested logit model, and the approach most widely used, is sequential estimation.

This estimation approach is based on the partitioning of the choice probability into a product of distinct multinomial logit models. The log likelihood of the model described above is

$$L = \sum_{n=1}^{N} \sum_{(r,t,w)\in C_n} y_{rtwn} \ln\left[P_n(r|tw) P_n(t|w) P_n(w)\right] \qquad 4.19$$

$$= \sum_{n=1}^{N} \sum_{r \in R_{nt^*w^*}} y_{rn} \ln P_n(r|t^*w^*)$$

$$+ \sum_{n=1}^{N} \sum_{t \in T_{nw^*}} y_{tn} \ln P_n(t|w^*) + \sum_{n=1}^{N} \sum_{w \in W_n} y_{wn} \ln P_n(w) \qquad 4.20$$

where

y_r = 1 if observation n chose residence location $r \in R_{nt^*w^*}$, 0 otherwise,

y_{tw^*} = 1 if observation n chose tenure $t \in T_{nw^*}$, 0 otherwise,

y_{wn} = 1 if observation n chose workplace $w \in W_n$, 0 otherwise, and

t^* and w^* represent the chosen tenure and workplace, respectively.

Once partitioned into the product of marginal and conditional choice probabilities in this way, each level of the model can be estimated by maximum likelihood. Model estimation proceeds from lower to higher level (conditional to marginal choice dimensions), with the estimated values of the inclusive values V'_{wt}, and V'_w, estimated from the first and second levels of the model, respectively, are included as independent variables in the estimation of the model in the next higher level. A detailed explanation of this sequential estimation method is provided by Ben-Akiva and Lerman (1987).

5 Results and interpretation

Model estimation results

The monocentric models of Alonso, Muth, and Mills, and the gravity models of Lowry, Wilson, and Putman, as well as most other models of residential location have been based on the assumption that the choice of workplace is the marginal choice in a household's decision hierarchy, and that residence location is determined as a conditional choice. Although much of the literature assumes a conditional choice structure in which the workplace is chosen first, housing tenure choice is subsequently made based on the chosen workplace, and residence location is made last, based on the chosen workplace and tenure, little systematic investigation of the validity of this assumption has been presented.

In this chapter we present the results of the estimation of a series of logit models of these three choice dimensions, designed to relax these restrictive assumptions regarding the nature and sequence of these household choice dimensions, and to allow for analysis of household behavior across these three choice dimensions. With a more integrated view of household behavior, it is hoped that the interacting impacts of public policies on household behavior can be more carefully examined.

Models were estimated for Black, Hispanic, and White non-Hispanic workers, with a total of 2,000 worker records in each sample. With 8 total alternatives for each worker (2 workplace, 2 tenure, 2 residence), the number of records in the estimation file were 16,000 per sample. Three alternative model structures were estimated for each population group:

1. a multinomial logit structure of the joint choice of workplace, tenure, and residence,

2. a two level nested logit structure with residence and tenure as the

joint conditional choice and workplace as the marginal choice, and

3   a three level nested logit structure with residence as a conditional choice based on the chosen workplace and tenure, with tenure as a conditional choice based on the chosen workplace, and workplace as the marginal choice.

The dependent variable in the joint logit specification is the joint probability that a worker will choose a particular combination of residence, workplace, and housing tenure. In the two-level nested logit, the dependent variable of the top level of the model is the probability that a worker will choose a particular workplace. The dependent variable in the second level of the two-level nested logit, then, is the joint probability that a worker will choose a particular combination of residence and tenure, given the prior choice of workplace. In the three-level nested logit specification, by extension, the dependent variables are, from higher to lower level, the probability that a worker will choose a particular workplace; the probability that a worker will choose a particular tenure given the prior choice of workplace; and the probability that a worker will choose a particular residence given the prior choices of workplace and tenure.

Table 5.1 provides definitions of the independent variables, and Tables 5.2, 5.3, and 5.4 provide the model estimation results for the joint, 2-level nested, and 3-level nested logit specifications, respectively.

Table 5.1 Variable definitions

Residence and Workplace

TIME	Travel time to work, in minutes
TIME2	Travel time to work squared

Residence Characteristics

DALCBD	Travel time from residence to Dallas CBD, in minutes
DALCBD2B	Travel time from residence to Dallas CBD squared
FWCBD	Travel time from residence to Fort Worth CBD, in minutes
FWCBD2	Travel time from residence to Fort Worth CBD squared
QHSNG	Share of regional total rental or owner housing supply
MNAGEAHU	Mean age of all housing units in residence zone
PCTBD	Percent of housing units boarded up in residence zone
PCTBLK	Percent Black population in residence zone
PCTSPN	Percent Hispanic population in residence zone
POPDEN	Population density in residence zone, in persons per acre
EMPDEN	Employment density in residence zone, in jobs per acre
INCBLK	Income of worker times percent Black population
INCSPN	Income of worker times percent Hispanic population
INCPHSNG	Income of worker times price of rental or owner-occupied housing
INCBEDR	Income of worker times average number of bedrooms in residence
AGEBLK	Age of worker times percent Black population
AGESPN	Age of worker times percent Hispanic population
AGEBEDR	Age of worker times average number of bedrooms in residence
NFAM	Non-family status of worker dummy times percent non-family households
FAMWC	Family status of worker dummy times percent family with children
AGE64	Worker over 64 dummy times percent of household heads over 64

Housing Tenure

OWN	Housing ownership alternative specific intercept (1 if owner)
INCOWN	Income of worker if homeowner, 0 otherwise
AGEOWN	Age of worker if homeowner, 0 otherwise
FAMOWN	1 if household is family with children and worker is homeowner
J_{ij}	Inclusive value from residence choice level of nested logit

Table 5.1 Continued

<u>Workplace Characteristics</u>

ED1SHR	Unskilled worker dummy times share of total unskilled jobs
ED2SHR	Low skilled worker dummy times share of total low skilled jobs
ED3SHR	Skilled worker dummy times share of total skilled jobs
ED4SHR	High skilled worker dummy times share of total high skilled jobs
WAGE1	Unskilled worker dummy times average wage for unskilled jobs
WAGE2	Low skilled worker dummy times average wage for low skilled jobs
WAGE3	Skilled worker dummy times average wage for skilled jobs
WAGE4	High skilled worker dummy times average wage for high skilled jobs
DALCBDW	Travel time in minutes from workplace to Dallas CBD
DALCBDW2	Travel time in minutes from workplace to Dallas CBD squared
FWCBDW	Travel time in minutes from workplace to Fort Worth CBD
FWCBDW2	Travel time in minutes from workplace to Fort Worth CBD squared
PCTBLK1	Unskilled worker dummy times percent black of unskilled workers
PCTBLK2	Low skilled worker dummy times percent black of low skilled workers
PCTBLK3	Skilled worker dummy times percent black of skilled workers
PCTBLK4	High skilled worker dummy times percent black of high skilled workers
PCTSPN1	Unskilled worker dummy times percent Hispanic of unskilled workers
PCTSPN2	Low skilled worker dummy times percent Hispanic of low skilled workers
PCTSPN3	Skilled worker dummy times percent Hispanic of skilled workers
PCTSPN4	High skilled worker dummy times percent Hispanic of high skilled workers
I_i	Inclusive value from tenure choice level of nested logit

Table 5.2 Model estimation results for 3-dimensional joint logit
Residence & Tenure & Workplace

	WHITE Coefficient	t Stat	BLACK Coefficient	t Stat	HISPANIC Coefficient	t Stat
Residence and Workplace						
TIME	-0.1020170	-33.882	-0.0853672	-21.115	-0.1057780	-35.39
TIME2	0.0002424	6.068	-0.0000738	-1.279	0.0002887	7.015
Residence Characteristics						
DALCBD	0.0513229	8.905	0.0851543	12.661	0.0882814	16.095
DALCBD2	-0.0002007	-3.414	-0.0009078	-11.538	-0.0005663	-9.857
FWCBD	0.0265087	4.857	0.0281969	4.143	0.0864266	15.849
FWCBD2	-0.0001470	-2.924	-0.0002823	-4.464	-0.0008163	-16.32
QHSNG	2.2107300	48.536	2.9525300	48.964	2.4548400	46.296
MNAGEAHU	-0.0076490	-3.925	-0.0363705	-14.099	0.0250669	12.292
PCTBD	-0.1963650	-6.391	-0.0902700	-18.856	-0.1473770	-12.326
PCTBLK	-0.0222592	-9.36	0.0290293	19.322	-0.0037620	-2.443
PCTSPN	-0.0139126	-3.718	0.0021583	0.567	0.0543583	23.394
POPDEN	0.0236796	5.715	0.0389494	9.769	0.0233035	6.438
EMPDEN	-0.0244072	-8.528	0.0031438	2.188	-0.0182065	-7.655
INCBLK	-0.0000008	-15.007	-0.0000004	-10.613	-0.0000004	-9.587
INCSPN	-0.0000015	-12.41	-0.0000012	-9.184	-0.0000010	-15.594
INCPHSNG	0.0000000	9.828	-0.0000000	6.312	0.0000000	3.36
INCBEDR	0.0000189	13.904	0.0000067	2.264	-0.0000000	-0.035
AGEBLK	0.0003045	5.923	0.0007412	18.511	0.0003501	8.392
AGESPN	0.0003570	3.959	0.0010149	10.667	0.0001300	2.099
AGEBEDR	-0.0126838	-13.342	-0.0025600	-1.864	-0.0028785	-2.469
NFAM	0.0230222	16.532	0.0070045	4.087	0.0220201	13.929
FAMWC	0.0223623	13.481	0.0320331	16.272	0.0206282	12.342
AGE64	0.0422674	7.112	0.0196567	2.366	0.0934697	7.046
Housing Tenure						
OWN	-3.7491000	-62.078	-4.3295300	-68.389	-4.0539300	-66.604
INCOWN	0.0000543	26.233	0.0000446	21.608	0.0000626	34.371
AGEOWN	0.0743563	51.677	0.0818054	59.638	0.0654423	44.966
FAMOWN	0.7709140	21.778	0.6688150	20.646	0.8542700	22.328

Table 5.2 Continued

Workplace Characteristics

ED1SHR	3.3186400	14.235	1.6872800	10.959	4.7112100	26.971
ED2SHR	3.1624800	23.068	1.3443000	20.433	1.4314500	17.464
ED3SHR	1.7013500	21.978	2.7387000	23.485	2.4420800	16.375
ED4SHR	7.1966400	16.189	33.8727000	6.885	13.9817000	6.758
WAGE1	0.0019720	5.132	0.0001621	0.38	0.0012599	3.574
WAGE2	0.0037369	12.054	0.0048600	13.929	0.0028210	9.878
WAGE3	0.0028000	13.05	0.0041582	15.6	0.0027393	12.397
WAGE4	0.0024172	8.673	-0.0011944	-3.767	-0.0000650	-0.243
DALCBDW	0.0072900	1.323	-0.0469991	-8.394	0.0037156	0.731
DALCBDW2	-0.0003062	-4.379	0.0007805	10.573	-0.0000397	-0.604
FWCBDW	-0.0290196	-5.034	-0.0145495	-2.282	-0.0208487	-3.698
FWCBDW2	0.0002008	3.546	0.0002671	4.183	0.0003120	5.564
PCTBLK1	-0.0242573	-6.468	-0.0029627	-0.965	-0.0148949	-6.086
PCTBLK2	-0.0042897	-1.139	0.0092677	3.61	-0.0030395	-0.849
PCTBLK3	-0.0152555	-5.041	0.0248449	8.145	-0.0097468	-2.654
PCTBLK4	-0.0434187	-8.796	0.1046340	11.033	0.0035282	0.451
PCTSPN1	0.0145582	1.668	0.0386860	4.137	0.0694720	13.875
PCTSPN2	0.0401287	5.514	-0.0129583	-1.722	0.0653983	8.516
PCTSPN3	0.0208289	3.236	-0.0205165	-2.417	0.0838722	10.721
PCTSPN4	-0.0318751	-2.651	0.0690098	5.386	0.0722071	3.719

Table 5.3 Model estimation results for 2-dimensional nested logit: residence / tenure / workplace

	WHITE Coefficient	t Stat	BLACK Coefficient	t Stat	HISPANIC Coefficient	t Stat
Residence and Workplace						
TIME	-0.0907399	-23.236	-0.1044650	-18.735	-0.0976323	-25.588
TIME2	0.0001046	2.098	0.0001306	1.743	0.0001784	3.48
Residence Characteristics						
DALCBD	0.0340723	4.925	0.0880790	10.531	0.0809002	12.233
DALCBD2	-0.0000055	-0.076	-0.0011295	-11.153	-0.0004066	-5.804
FWCBD	0.0130343	1.958	-0.0076458	-0.862	0.0866583	13.065
FWCBD2	-0.0000085	-0.138	0.0000398	0.488	-0.0007788	-12.806
QHSNG	2.4068900	46.375	4.1062100	50.961	2.7080400	42.759
MNAGEAHU	-0.0017025	-0.73	-0.0301978	-9.696	0.0247707	10.152
PCTBD	-0.2122280	-5.706	-0.0724576	-14.115	-0.1468960	-11.516
PCTBLK	-0.0260041	-9.058	0.0255295	13.784	-0.0011572	-0.627
PCTSPN	0.0101524	2.083	-0.0000417	-0.009	0.0579402	20.304
POPDEN	0.0191645	3.855	0.0179197	3.711	0.0230071	5.236
EMPDEN	-0.0286514	-8.189	0.0028115	1.396	-0.0155171	-5.757
INCBLK	-0.0000006	-6.916	-0.0000003	-6.737	-0.0000005	-10.087
INCSPN	-0.0000019	-11.644	-0.0000013	-8.258	-0.0000010	-13.862
INCPHSNG	0.0000000	5.195	-0.0000000	-4.932	0.0000000	2.182
INCBEDR	0.0000260	11.86	0.0000035	0.988	-0.0000012	-0.959
AGEBLK	0.0002923	4.778	0.0007564	15.526	0.0003120	6.428
AGESPN	-0.0001434	-1.302	0.0012563	10.136	0.0000110	0.147
AGEBEDR	-0.0175452	-13.684	-0.0011960	-0.733	-0.0021932	-1.651
NFAM	0.0207402	12.387	-0.0042400	-1.975	0.0167425	9.035
FAMWC	0.0262260	13.081	0.0362344	15.255	0.0203962	10.122
AGE64	0.0412937	5.475	0.0073159	0.756	0.0326495	1.98
Housing Tenure						
OWN	-3.7082800	-61.119	-4.2451500	-66.012	-4.0690600	-66.128
INCOWN	0.0000522	22.689	0.0000443	20.193	0.0000634	34.683
AGEOWN	0.0755117	50.173	0.0814801	57.774	0.0655164	44.183
FAMOWN	0.7619690	21.376	0.6204530	18.82	0.8580090	22.122

Table 5.3 Continued

Workplace Characteristics

ED1SHR	3.2111000	13.637	1.6839200	10.958	4.7575200	26.639
ED2SHR	3.1990800	22.867	1.3699700	19.044	1.4079600	17.274
ED3SHR	1.6959300	21.364	2.5422400	23.334	2.4126600	16.261
ED4SHR	7.6639600	17.657	36.6937000	7.59	14.1460000	6.59
WAGE1	0.0019747	5.089	0.0002736	0.667	0.0011677	3.289
WAGE2	0.0037203	11.66	0.0046190	13.638	0.0027231	9.398
WAGE3	0.0028358	12.72	0.0042776	16.761	0.0028047	12.624
WAGE4	0.0024940	8.794	-0.0009717	-3.127	-0.0000790	-0.287
DALCBDW	0.0085762	1.519	-0.0443454	-7.992	0.0035959	0.705
DALCBDW2	-0.0003283	-4.462	0.0007156	9.527	-0.0000591	-0.88
FWCBDW	-0.0296690	-5.007	-0.0141433	-2.307	-0.0203622	-3.592
FWCBDW2	0.0002079	3.631	0.0002618	4.203	0.0002945	5.23
PCTBLK1	-0.0252571	-6.215	-0.0010868	-0.365	-0.0145359	-5.892
PCTBLK2	-0.0062278	-1.645	0.0073682	2.961	-0.0035114	-0.968
PCTBLK3	-0.0148440	-4.902	0.0234205	7.826	-0.0109985	-2.952
PCTBLK4	-0.0460911	-8.929	0.1013160	11.478	0.0057933	0.699
PCTSPN1	0.0136870	1.438	0.0353378	4.031	0.0712780	14.017
PCTSPN2	0.0387075	5.355	-0.0118206	-1.627	0.0652627	8.399
PCTSPN3	0.0201595	3.104	-0.0201300	-2.413	0.0835435	10.643
PCTSPN4	-0.0359189	-2.922	0.0606940	4.922	0.0752303	3.79
J_{ij}	1.0011500	50.429	0.9014970	58.296	1.0237600	55.181

Table 5.4 Model estimation results for 3-dimensional nested logit: residence / tenure / workplace

	WHITE Coefficient	t Stat	BLACK Coefficient	t Stat	HISPANIC Coefficient	t Stat
Residence and Workplace						
TIME	-0.0904378	-22.614	-0.0929638	-17.196	-0.0997370	-26.038
TIME2	0.0000867	1.7	0.0000576	0.786	0.0002289	4.428
Residence Characteristics						
DALCBD	0.0261773	3.668	0.0865768	10.621	0.0875606	13.185
DALCBD2	0.0000620	0.826	-0.0010216	-10.296	-0.0004886	-6.943
FWCBD	0.0006870	0.099	0.0014046	0.163	0.0875082	13.198
FWCBD2	0.0001163	1.812	-0.0000053	-0.067	-0.0007951	-13.076
QHSNG	3.5233200	31.637	2.3655400	23.742	2.4711500	24.031
MNAGEAHU	0.0024873	1.008	-0.0399800	-13.072	0.0197249	7.975
PCTBD	-0.2187350	-5.458	-0.0718748	-14.457	-0.1507130	-11.578
PCTBLK	-0.0279188	-9.401	0.0253398	14.111	-0.0018081	-0.968
PCTSPN	0.0124663	2.439	0.0148236	3.131	0.0592540	20.693
POPDEN	0.0126994	2.445	0.0354664	7.602	0.0298467	6.668
EMPDEN	-0.0311159	-8.386	-0.0012488	-0.622	-0.0161712	-5.809
INCBLK	-0.0000005	-5.993	-0.0000003	-7.467	-0.0000005	-9.136
INCSPN	-0.0000021	-11.901	-0.0000016	-9.609	-0.0000008	-12.817
INCPHSNG	0.0000000	4.69	-0.0000000	-3.309	0.0000000	4.916
INCBEDR	0.0000194	8.328	0.0000027	0.657	-0.0000007	-0.367
AGEBLK	0.0003068	4.904	0.0006955	14.625	0.0003238	6.512
AGESPN	-0.0001827	-1.584	0.0007779	6.246	-0.0000170	-0.224
AGEBEDR	-0.0128498	-8.27	-0.0142005	-6.288	-0.0012653	-0.726
NFAM	0.0227449	12.634	-0.0031474	-1.387	0.0184482	9.662
FAMWC	0.0235231	10.727	0.0372885	15.324	0.0147593	6.788
AGE64	0.0325007	4.283	-0.0017385	-0.167	0.0285658	1.785
Housing Tenure						
OWN	-3.7175600	-61.901	-4.1374500	-60.812	-4.0597200	-64.496
INCOWN	0.0000599	30.065	0.0000489	11.099	0.0000620	30.117
AGEOWN	0.0697136	49.555	0.0903021	38.978	0.0655264	38.338
FAMOWN	0.8081180	22.657	0.5455720	15.38	0.8564220	21.526
J_{ij}	0.5591240	28.748	2.2656800	29.118	1.2028000	25.032

Table 5.4 Continued

Workplace Characteristics

ED1SHR	3.1102900	12.874	1.6515000	10.932	4.7771100	26.862
ED2SHR	3.2142400	21.54	1.3304800	19.966	1.4066900	17.296
ED3SHR	1.6523900	19.881	2.7298600	23.941	2.4185600	16.237
ED4SHR	7.2306100	15.545	40.0024000	8.057	14.0940000	6.599
WAGE1	0.0019941	4.994	-0.0000112	-0.027	0.0011327	3.188
WAGE2	0.0037614	10.957	0.0046004	13.249	0.0027223	9.411
WAGE3	0.0028946	12.124	0.0043018	16.285	0.0027594	12.444
WAGE4	0.0023888	8.008	-0.0011335	-3.559	-0.0001219	-0.44
DALCBDW	0.0071384	1.187	-0.0422430	-7.624	0.0040940	0.804
DALCBDW2	-0.0003095	-3.764	0.0007210	9.894	-0.0000593	-0.889
FWCBDW	-0.0317959	-4.929	-0.0086691	-1.386	-0.0198380	-3.501
FWCBDW2	0.0002272	3.746	0.0002081	3.3	0.0002938	5.231
PCTBLK1	-0.0263304	-5.557	0.0000134	0.004	-0.0145785	-5.905
PCTBLK2	-0.0068351	-1.779	0.0088966	3.49	-0.0031813	-0.882
PCTBLK3	-0.0137132	-4.322	0.0238636	7.959	-0.0093366	-2.499
PCTBLK4	-0.0424098	-7.713	0.1111430	13.107	0.0028955	0.338
PCTSPN1	0.0143205	1.308	0.0372136	4.06	0.0727501	14.294
PCTSPN2	0.0365599	4.988	-0.0140752	-1.876	0.0664833	8.596
PCTSPN3	0.0193121	2.819	-0.0205501	-2.465	0.0844247	10.714
PCTSPN4	-0.0426791	-3.36	0.0642924	4.97	0.0726845	3.636
Ii	1.6654900	22.539	0.4715120	34.936	0.8735670	26.334

The following table provides summary goodness-of-fit statistics for the preceding models:

Table 5.5 Summary measures of goodness-of-fit for estimated models

	WHITE	BLACK	HISPANIC
JOINT LOGIT			
Log-Likelihood	-23798	-24052	-27933
Chi-Squared	56106	69734	-56997
Degrees of Freedom	47	47	47
2-LEVEL NESTED LOGIT			
Tenure & Residence Choice			
Log-Likelihood	-18076	-19083	-21693
Chi-Squared	32982	40392	32610
Degrees of Freedom	27	27	27
Workplace Choice			
Log-Likelihood	-5851	-5218	-6301
Chi-Squared	22865	28842	25397
Degrees of Freedom	21	21	21
Combined 2-Level Nested			
Log-Likelihood	-23927	-24301	-27994
3-LEVEL NESTED LOGIT			
Residence Choice			
Log-Likelihood	-7031	-5758	-8116
Chi-Squared	20506	27764	21767
Degrees of Freedom	23	23	23
Tenure Choice			
Log-Likelihood	-11004	-13363	-13581
Chi-Squared	12560	12553	10837
Degrees of Freedom	5	5	5
Workplace Choice			
Log-Likelihood	-5898	-4868	-6284
Chi-Squared	22771	29544	25431
Degrees of Freedom	21	21	21
Combined 3-Level Nested			
Log-Likelihood	-23933	-23989	-27981

Model specification alternatives

Before beginning an interpretation of the individual coefficients of the models, we touch briefly on the preferred model structure. As noted earlier, three choice sequences were evaluated for the model structure: all three dimensions as a joint choice, a two-level hierarchical choice in which the joint choice of residence location and housing tenure is made based on a marginal choice of workplace location, and a three-level hierarchical structure in which residence location is chosen based on the choice of housing tenure, which is chosen on the basis of the chosen workplace.

Two techniques were used to evaluate these alternative model structures. The first is the value of the inclusive values on the nested logit models. Theoretically acceptable ranges for the inclusive values are 0 to 1, with a value of 1 indicating that the model reduces to the special case of a joint choice, or simple multinomial logit model. In the 2-level nested logit case, the values of the inclusive value are 1.00 for whites, 0.90 for blacks, and 1.02 for Hispanics. This range of values would strongly argue for a joint logit specification, with blacks being the closest to warranting a nested logit structure.

In the three-level nested logit structure, the value of the inclusive values at the second level (tenure choice) are .56 for whites, 2.26 for blacks, and 1.20 for Hispanics, and for the third level (workplace choice), the values are 1.66, 0.47, and 0.87, respectively. This pattern of values falls outside the range considered theoretically acceptable, and would tend to reject the use of a three level nested structure.

The second technique for comparing the model structures is by comparing the sum of the log-likelihoods of the alternative model structures. The model with the smallest absolute value of the log-likelihood is considered to have the best fit. For whites and Hispanics, the joint logit model slightly outperformed the two- and three-level nested specifications, and for Blacks the three-level performed slightly better, but the three-level nested logit was excluded based on the out-of-range inclusive values.

Interpretation of results

As a result of the two tests described in the prior section, we select the joint logit specification as the preferred model structure (see Table 5.2). In the following sections, the coefficients from the joint logit model are examined in detail for whites, blacks, and Hispanics, separately by choice dimension.

Before beginning a detailed review of the model results, a brief summary of the interpretation of the model coefficients is in order. Recall that the dependent variable in the selected joint choice model is the combined probability that a white, black, or Hispanic worker will choose to reside in a given census tract, will choose to work in a given census tract (not necessary the same one in which he/she resides), and will choose to own or rent his/her home. The fact that the probability is a joint choice implies that, across whites as a group, or blacks, or Hispanics, we assume that the choices of residence, workplace, and housing tenure are not totally independent, but may, in fact, influence each other. While for a given individual these decisions are not assumed to be made simultaneously, we simply assume that across all individuals, we cannot determine a definite sequence to the decisions, so they are evaluated in the model as joint choices.

The sign of the coefficients can be interpreted simply as indicating whether a particular variable increases or decreases the probability that a particular combination of residence, workplace, and housing tenure alternatives will be chosen. While the variables are grouped into different components of the workers' utility expressions, reflecting their primary influence on one particular dimension of choice, such as residence choice, the joint logit model allows a particular variable or combination of variables influence the probability not only of that choice dimension, but of all three choice dimensions.

To clarify, a coefficient of -.196 on the variable PCTBD (the percent of the housing units in a census tract which are boarded up), indicates that increasing the proportion of boarded up, abandoned housing in a census tract, holding all other characteristics of the census tract constant, holding constant all other characteristics of tenure and workplace choice, and most importantly, holding constant the percent of housing boarded up in all alternative census tracts, will reduce the joint probability of choosing that residence tract, housing tenure, and workplace tract. We would attribute most or all of the reduced joint probability to a reduction in the probability of choosing the census tract for residence, but we can not rule out a potential negative influence on the probability of owning as opposed to renting as the level of housing abandonment increases.

A second example further clarifies the interpretation of the coefficients. The variables TIME and TIME2 are a quadratic expression of a travel time function between residence and workplace, in minutes. If we evaluate the expression at a variety of travel times, we typically find a downward sloping function of travel time. This can be interpreted to mean that as travel time increases for a given alternative combination of residence and workplace - as compared to all alternative residence-workplace combinations, the probability that a worker will choose that combination of residence, workplace, and tenure will decrease. In this case, we clearly cannot attribute the reduced joint probability solely to one of the choice dimensions. The journey to work travel time is a function of the **relationship between residence and workplace**, so an increase in travel time - from increased congestion, for example - would reduce the attractiveness not specifically of the particular residence location or workplace location, but of the unique combination of residence and workplace which generate that travel time. The increased travel time may also affect the housing tenure probability, since homeowners are typically less sensitive to longer commutes than renters.

In the next several sections, we review in detail the coefficients of the joint choice model presented in Table 5.2, grouping the discussion according to the three choice dimensions: residence, tenure, and workplace. Note that in the joint logit specification, the effect of an independent variable may apply to more than one of the choice dimensions, and the interpretation of the effect must therefore be made cautiously.

Choice of residence location

As noted earlier, there are five dominant factors which are hypothesized to influence the pattern of residential locations. These are: accessibility to the workplace, physical characteristics of the housing stock, race and ethnicity, socioeconomic status, and stage of life cycle. We examine each of these influences in turn, with the exception of the journey to work travel time variables. The discussion of the journey to work follows discussion of the workplace variables, since as already noted, travel time affects residence and workplace choice in combination.

Residential suburbanization The variables measuring the distance (in minutes of travel time) from the Dallas and Fort Worth CBD's are DALCBD, DALCBD2, FWCBD and FWCBD2. Quadratic forms were used, since travel decay and urban density functions are generally found to have nonlinear forms. These variables are evaluated as quadratic functions, and plotted against travel time to the two CBD's in figures 5.1 and 5.2.

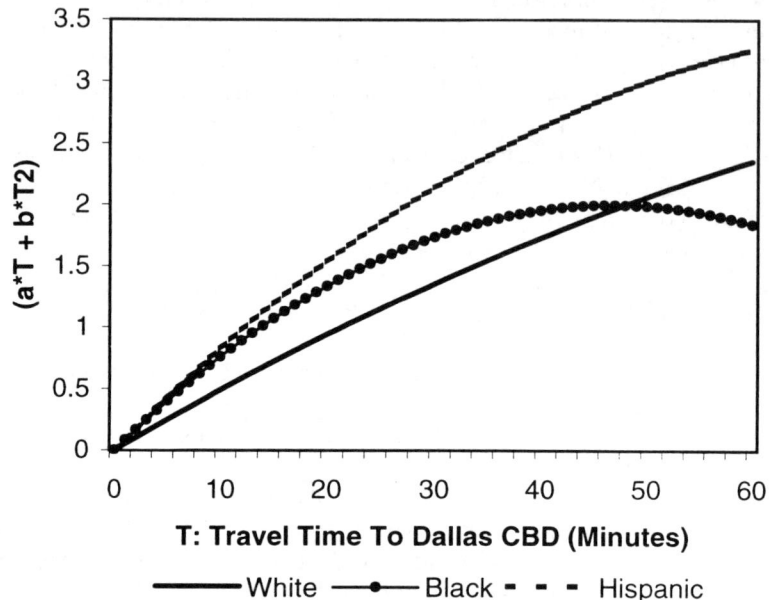

Figure 5.1 Function of distance from Dallas CBD

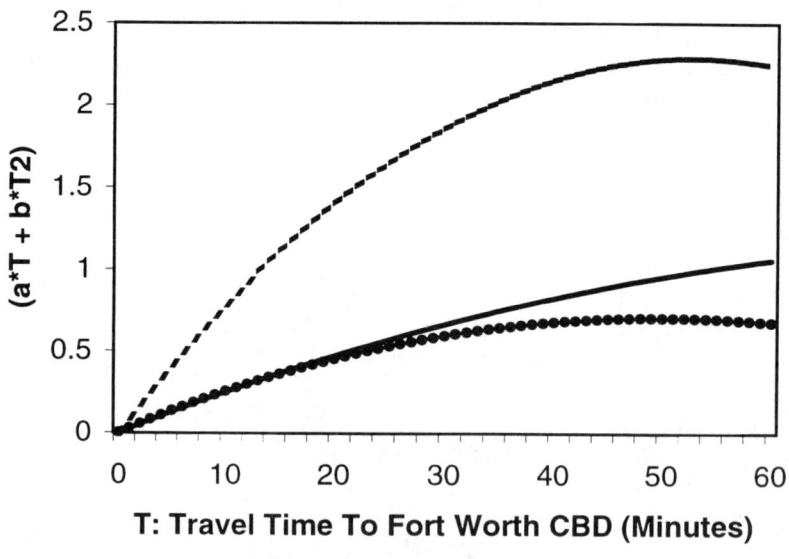

Figure 5.2 Function of distance from Fort Worth CBD

The pattern for the two CBD's is rather similar, although there appear to be significant differences between the population groups. Whites reveal a positive and consistently increasing relationship with travel time from the Dallas CBD, and a similar positive relationship with travel time to the Fort Worth CBD, although the function has a lower trajectory in Tarrant County. This pattern reflects the expected suburbanization tendency among whites, and the relatively low proportions of whites who choose to live in the central cities, close to the commercial centers of the metropolitan area, and the associated poverty, crime, and racial integration. Blacks and Hispanics also show an increasing function of distance from the CBD's, but with larger negative coefficients on the exponential terms, the decentralization effect tends to taper off as as the travel time approaches one hour, and for blacks, begins decreasing with respect to the Dallas CBD. The function for blacks also tends to lie at a lower level at each point than that for Hispanics.

The negative coefficients on the exponential terms for blacks and Hispanics are significantly larger than for whites, resulting in a downturn of the suburbanization function beyond the 60 minute travel time radius plotted in the foregoing figures, but we would tend to consider these functions somewhat nonsensical at such extreme distances (the maximum potential travel time from one tract to another within the study area is approximately 120 minutes, and average travel time is less than 30 minutes). Two considerations are important in interpreting these results, however. First, the variables representing travel time of residence to the Dallas CBD provide an additive effect with the variables representing distance from the residence to the Fort Worth CBD.

The second consideration is that the distance variables from the CBD are symmetrical with respect to the CBD, therefore averaging the function for each population group across sectors with high and low concentrations of that population group. To clarify, blacks in Dallas County are predominantly located in a wedge located to the south of the central business district. A variable describing the probability of choosing a residence as a function of distance from the Dallas CDB which analyzed only tracts to the north of the CBD would show a very different shape than a function measured south of the CBD. For blacks, which tend to be highly segregated residentially within sectors of both Dallas and Tarrant Counties, a symmetrical function with respect to the CBD results in a function which is significantly flatter might be expected from examining maps of the residential distribution of blacks. Other variables in the model pick up the segregation effect (ie. the percent black population in each tract), and in essence, overlay this effect on the symmetrical residential suburbanization functions.

Population and Employment Density   Two other variables which are correlated with distance from the CBD are the densities of population and employment.

POPDEN, measured in persons per acre, has almost identical coefficients for whites and Hispanics, at 0.023 and 0.023, respectively, with t-statistics of 5.7 and 6.4. These coefficients indicate that the probability of choosing a census tract is positively associated with the population density of that tract, all else being constant. This is the reciprocal of stating that few persons reside in areas of very low population density (ie. rural areas) within the study area. Blacks have a significantly higher coefficient of 0.039, with a t-statistic of 9.8. This is not an unexpected result, given the residential segregation of blacks in high density core areas near the CBD's, and particularly high density public housing projects.

EMPDEN, measured as the number of jobs per acre (at the workplace), has similar negative coefficients for whites and Hispanics, at -0.024 and -0.018, with t-statistics of -8.5 and -7.7. This is consistent with an aversion to residential locations which are dominated by commercial activity, due to externalities such as traffic, noise, and pollution. Blacks, on the other hand, register a positive coefficient of 0.0031, with a t-statistic of 2.1. Again, this result must be attributed to the segregation of blacks and their low incomes, and not to their preference to reside in high density commercial areas with all of the associated disamenities of those locations.

Residential density gradients The findings here regarding the housing supply, population and employment density, and proximity to the CBD's are consistent with the residential density gradients of Mills (1972) and Muth (1969), but provide a more explicit view of the components of the density gradients measured by Mills and Muth - and highlight significant differences between whites, blacks, and Hispanics. For comparative purposes, we calculate residential density gradients for each population group and for total population, for Dallas County, Tarrant County, and the combined metropolitan 2-county area. Since there are two central cities and two CBD's, in the combined analysis, we use the distance to the nearest CBD. The density function used is the familiar exponential function $D(x) = D_o e^{-bx}$ where $D(x)$ is the population density (in persons per acre) x miles from the city center, e is the base of the natural logarithm, D_0 is the density at the city center, and b is the density gradient. Table 5.6 summarizes our findings:

Table 5.6 Population density gradients

Geographic Scope	Total	White	Black	Hispanic
2-County	-.115*	.011	-.290*	-.186*
Dallas County	-.125*	.027	-.314*	-.177*
Tarrant County	-.105*	-.047	-.303*	-.216*

* Significant at the 5 percent level

These results closely mirror the results of our model estimation, with blacks having the steepest density gradient, Hispanics showing approximately two thirds the density gradient of blacks, and whites showing relatively flat and insignificant density gradients, indicating the advanced degree of white suburbanization within the two county area: white population density actually increases with distance from the CBD in the Dallas County and 2-county case. Two elements may account for these striking racial and ethnic differences: first, the differences in average socioeconomic status, which are translated into divergent levels of suburbanization, and second, differing abilities to translate socioeconomic gains into suburbanization, as documented by Massey (1984).

Housing Supply The overall supply of housing at each location regulates the residential location potential at each location, and is therefore a dominant conditioning variable in the choice of residential location. The housing supply variable, QHSNG, has highly significant positive coefficients for whites, blacks, and Hispanics. The coefficients are quite similar for the three groups, varying from 2.21 for whites to 2.45 for Hispanics, and 2.95 for blacks. The t-statistics for these coefficients are almost identical, at 48.5, 46.3, and 48.9 for whites, blacks, and Hispanics. It is likely that some of the remaining variance in the probability of choosing residential locations for each group, after inclusion in the model of the other characteristics of residential locations, may be picked up by this housing supply variable. In other words, as additional detail on the texture and complexity of residential choice is captured in the model by better specification, the coefficient on the housing supply variable would be expected to reduce to a minimum level which would represent simply a supply constraint on residential location.

Housing Age Higher age of the housing stock in each census tract is found to reduce the probability that whites and blacks will choose to reside there, but Hispanics are found to have a positive coefficient on the variable MNAGEAHU. The coefficients for whites, blacks, and Hispanics are -.007, -.036, and 0.025, respectively, with t-statistics of -3.9, -14.1, and 12.3.

Housing Quality Socioeconomic status is the most obvious influence on the choice of housing quality and quantity. We find significant differences between whites, blacks, and Hispanics in terms of their income distributions, as shown in Table 5.7.

Table 5.7 Annual earnings by race (1979 $)

	White	Black	Hispanic
Under $10,000	36%	58%	53%
$10,000-$19,999	36%	35%	35%
$20,000-$29,999	17%	6%	9%
$30,000-$39,999	5%	1%	2%
$40,000-$49,999	2%	0%	1%
$50,000-$59,999	1%	0%	0%
$60,000 or more	3%	0%	0%

The earnings distribution of both blacks and Hispanics is clearly skewed towards the lower end, as compared to that of whites. Black workers are slightly more likely to earn less than $10,000 than are Hispanic workers, and slightly less likely to earn more than $20,000. The most substantial, though expected difference lies between whites and the other two groups for earnings of less than $10,000, where there is a twenty point gap in the distribution. These income differences influence our interpretation of the housing quality variables below.

The prevalence of substandard housing is measured by PCTBD, the percent of housing units which are boarded up. As expected, all three groups have a significant aversion to locations which have a high proportion of dilapidated housing, with coefficients on PCTBD of -.196, -.09, and -.147 for whites, blacks, and Hispanics, with t-statistics of -6.3, -18.9, and -12.3. The higher incomes of whites appear to provide them with ample resources to avoid areas with high concentrations of substandard housing. Hispanics, however, are almost as able to avoid such areas as are whites, even though the income distribution of Hispanics is almost the same as that of blacks. The comparatively low ability of blacks to avoid areas high in substandard housing cannot, therefore, be attributed solely to a lack of income.

The influence of the average size of home at each residential location, as measured by the average number of bedrooms, is captured by INCBEDR and AGEBEDR, representing the income and age interaction with the size of housing, respectively. These interaction terms between the income and age of the household and the average number of bedrooms in homes within each tract, behave for the most part as expected. INCBEDR is significant and positive for whites and blacks, with coefficients of .000019 and .000007, and t-statistics of 13.9 and 2.3, respectively. This indicates that as incomes rise, white and black households tend to choose larger homes, as would be expected if housing is a normal good. Hispanics, on the other hand, have an insignificant coefficient on this variable, without the expected sign. This is potentially due to a negative correlation between the age of housing, on which Hispanics had a positive coefficient, and the size of housing.

The age interaction with the size of housing behaves as expected for all three groups, with negative coefficients on AGEBEDR of -.013, -.003, and -.003 for whites, blacks, and Hispanics, respectively. The t-statistics are -13.3, -1.86, and -2.47 for the three groups. The larger coefficient for whites could reflect the relatively greater mobility of whites into smaller homes in more central areas once they have completed their childrearing and the nuclear family has dissolved.

The income interaction with housing is captured by the variable INCPHSNG, an interaction between the income of the household and the average price of housing at each residential location. The coefficient on this variable is 0.000000014 for whites, -0.000000031 for blacks, and 0.000000008 for Hispanics, with t-statistics of 9.8, -6.3, and 3.4, respectively. While housing would be expected to be considered a normal good by all groups, and therefore to have a positive coefficient, the coefficient on this variable is positive for whites, smaller but still positive for Hispanics, and negative for blacks.

This result could indicate that blacks pay less for housing than whites and Hispanics, a finding which would be consistent with Berry's (1976) findings that excess housing construction (above the level of demand) in the Chicago housing market led to accelerated housing filtering, and lower prices for blacks. Alternatively, this result could obtain if blacks are excluded from more expensive housing through discrimination by whites. These interpretations may not be inconsistent, if in a soft housing market, with underlying racial prejudice, overt discrimination recedes as housing filtering and racial succession (white flight) increases - while in a tight housing market, racial prejudice gives way to overt discrimination as whites face diminishing opportunities to move to new housing at the periphery and instead defend their neighborhoods from 'invasion'. The likelihood that the mechanism of housing filtering is at work without an underlying foundation of prejudice seems remote based on the additional evidence provided in the following sections.

Residential segregation No model of residential location would be credible without incorporating race as an influence on residential choice. It is no surprise that the Dallas-Fort Worth area, like almost every other urban area in the United States, is highly segregated racially. The degree to which race determines residential location is nevertheless quite startling. Murdock (1982) has calculated the Taueber and Taueber (1965) two-group indices of dissimilarity for cities in Texas. We report his calculations for the two central cities of Dallas and Fort Worth in our study area for 1970 and 1980 in Table 5.8, using both census tracts and census blocks. Values approaching 0 would indicate total integration, while those approaching 1 indicate nearly complete residential segregation.

Table 5.8 Residential segregation in 1970 and 1980

	Anglo vs. Black		Anglo vs. Hispanic		Black vs. Hispanic	
	1970	1980	1970	1980	1970	1980
Census Tracts						
Dallas	.93	.80	.45	.55	.82	.72
Ft. Worth	.84	.79	.49	.55	.79	.73
Census Blocks						
Dallas	.83	.85	.59	.64	.78	.81
Ft. Worth	.86	.87	.62	.65	.86	.86

These indices reveal that the level of white-black segregation is quite high in both years, both cities, and both levels of aggregation. The level of white-Hispanic segregation is significantly less, and the level of black-Hispanic segregation is almost as high as the level of white-black segregation. There are differences in the results at the tract and the block levels, as would be expected since the borders of segregated areas may be quite localized. Although the tract level indices show white-black segregation declining between 1970 and 1980, the block level indices show this level increasing slightly. At both levels, the white-Hispanic level of segregation is shown to be increasing, and the levels of black-Hispanic segregation are ambiguous in their direction.

The variables PCTBLK, PCTSPN, INCBLK, INCSPN, AGEBLK, and AGESPN in our model provide a revealing view of the degree to which race influences residential location in Dallas-Fort Worth, and provide insight into the root causes for the documented levels of segregation. The variables represent the percent of the population of each tract which are black or Hispanic, and the income and age interaction with the percent black and Hispanic. The PCTBLK and PCTSPN variables could be interpreted as constant terms in functions which include income and age interactions with the percent black and Hispanic. In other words, the PCTBLK and PCTSPN are the base effects, or intercepts, of these functions, and the slopes are determined by the income and age interactions.

The coefficient for whites on PCTBLK are -.022, with a t-statistic of -9.4. This represents an aversion to areas which contain significant proportions of black population. This result is underscored by a negative income interaction with percent black, with the coefficient of INCBLK of -.0000009, and a t-statistic of -15.0. The age interaction with percent black, however, had a positive coefficient of .0003, with a t-statistic of 5.9, which is consistent with the observation of black ghetto expansion into adjacent areas of older white residents as the housing in those neighborhoods becomes available through attrition of the white residents.

The coefficient for blacks on PCTBLK are positive at 0.029, with a t-statistic of 19.3. This positive coefficient must be interpreted, in isolation, as the result partly of clustering among blacks by preference, through the process of subcultural intensification described by Berry (1973), and partly as a result of housing discrimination or other means of exclusion by whites from predominantly white areas. The variable, by itself, cannot provide much information about the relative contribution of these two influences. When this variable is examined in combination with the income interaction with the percent black, for blacks, however, the interpretation becomes clearer. The coefficient on INCBLK for blacks is significant and negative, at -.0000005, with a t-statistic of -10.6. This indicates that blacks prefer to avoid the extreme segregation which exists in the core of the black ghettoes of Dallas and Fort Worth, and attempt to move away from the highest black concentrations of the ghetto core if their income allows them to. There appears to be a segregation within the black community along socioeconomic lines, with wealthier blacks moving to the periphery of the black areas, or moving out altogether and 'mainstreaming' into mostly white areas.

The positive coefficient on AGEBLK of .0007, with a t-statistic of 4.1, is consistent with the concentration of older blacks, many of whom are quite poor, in ghetto areas which are predominantly black. It is also consistent with the preference of younger, better educated black households to separate themselves from the core of the ghetto within the black community, or to flee the black community altogether. One could argue, perhaps, that the black residential areas are an historical artifact, and that these results indicate that young blacks are freeing themselves from the ghetto. A cursory examination of the residential distribution of blacks suggests, however, that the residential isolation of blacks largely persists as of 1980, in spite of the preferences of younger and wealthier blacks to avoid segregation.

Hispanics reflect an aversion to black population concentrations, with a coefficient on PCTBLK of -.0038, and a t-statistic of -2.44. While this is smaller than the coefficient of whites on this variable, it may reflect the inability of the lowest income Hispanics to avoid ghetto residential locations. The income interaction of Hispanics with the percent black, INCBLK, is -.00000046, with a t-statistic of -9.6, revealing an aversion to black population concentrations as income rises. It is of note, however, that the income interaction is almost identical between blacks and Hispanics, but the coefficient on income interaction for whites is twice as large, further documenting the degree of white avoidance of black population. The age interaction of Hispanics with the percent black population is similar to that of whites, with a coefficient of 0.00035, and a t-statistic of 8.4.

Whites express an aversion to concentrations of Hispanic as well as to black population, with a coefficient on PCTSPN of -0.0139, and a t-statistic of -3.7.

The income interaction of whites with Hispanic population is also negative, with a coefficient of -0.0000015, and a t-statistic of -12.4. While the size of the coefficient on PCTSPN is smaller than the coefficient on PCTBLK, the income interaction is larger on INCSPN than on INCBLK. This may reflect a higher degree of integration among whites of lower income with Hispanics than with blacks, thus requiring a relatively larger income effect to provide whites with their desired level of residential ethnic homogeneity at higher income levels. The age interaction with percent Hispanic population, AGESPN, has a coefficient of 0.00036, with a t-statistic of 3.96. This is similar in magnitude to AGEBLK, and most likely results from neighborhood turnover from older whites to Hispanics.

Blacks have an insignificant coefficient on PCTSPN, with a t-statistic of only 0.57. The income interaction, INCSPN, however, is negative, with a coefficient of -0.0000013, and a t-statistic of -9.2. This combination is a plausible result if low income blacks and Hispanics are forced by a limited supply of low income housing to reside in close proximity, such as in public housing concentrations, but begin to segregate as higher income provides opportunities to realize a preference for segregation through residential mobility. The age interaction with percent Hispanic, AGESPN, is positive for blacks, with a coefficient of 0.001, and a t-statistic of 10.7. This result may be due to lower mobility of the elderly population, as neighborhoods undergo transformation from one ethnic group to another.

Hispanics have a positive coefficient on PCTSPN of 0.054, with a t-statistic of 23.4. Their income interaction with percent Hispanic population, however, is negative, with a coefficient on INCSPN of -0.000001, and a t-statistic of -15.6. Although the negative income interaction reveals a preference to avoid high levels of ethnic segregation, the income interaction of Hispanics on the percent Hispanic is smaller than that for whites and blacks, indicating stronger preferences by those two ethnic groups to avoid residential concentrations of Hispanic population. The age interaction of Hispanics with the percent Hispanic is positive and significant, with a coefficient of 0.00013 and a t-statistic of 2.1, but this coefficient is much smaller and less significant than those on the same variable for blacks and whites. This is a plausible result if the areas with high densities of Hispanic population - the barrios - are dominated by fairly recent immigrants with a young age structure and high birth rates.

Life Cycle Differentiation Three variables are included in the model to capture the degree to which the stage of life cycle acts as a segregating influence on residential choice. Before reviewing the coefficients, we provide a tabulation of the population at risk of being included in our sample, by type of household, in Table 5.9 to identify average differences between the three population groups. Recall that our sample excludes married couple households in which both husband and wife work, in order to minimize the distortions caused by multiple earner households.

Table 5.9 Workers by household type

	White	Black	Hispanic
Husband-Wife Family			
Only Husband Works	40%	25%	53%
Only Wife Works	0%	1%	0%
Male Householder	3%	6%	7%
Female Householder	11%	31%	11%
Non-Family	45%	38%	29%

Black workers are significantly less likely to be husbands in a 'traditional' married couple family household in which only the husband works, and are three times more likely to be female heads of families than whites or Hispanics. Hispanics have a relatively low probability of being in a non-family household, and a compensating high probability of being in the 'traditional' married couple family in which only the husband works. These differences may arise from a combination of differences in age structures, socioeconomic status, cultural values, and the impact of welfare regulations, and are likely to shape the degree to which these groups cluster by stage of life cycle.

The variable NFAM is the interaction between a dummy variable for non-family household status of the chooser, with the percent of the households in each census tract which are non-family. The coefficient for whites is positive and significant, with a value of 0.023 and a t-statistic of 16.5. This reflects a positive sorting of population by household status, with non-family households clustering in denser, more centrally located residential communities than child-rearing family households. The coefficient on NFAM for blacks is 0.007, and for Hispanics, 0.022, with t-statistics of 4.1 and 13.9, respectively. The coefficients on this variable for whites and Hispanics are almost identical, but blacks have a much lower and less significant coefficient. The similarity between whites and Hispanics, and the difference between blacks and the other two groups, obtains in spite of the fact that the proportion of black workers which are non-family lies halfway between the proportion for the other two groups.

Although not conclusive, this result is consistent an underrepresentation of non-family blacks in the apartment communities populated by white and hispanic non-family households, potentially the result of some form of direct discrimination by landlords, owners, managers, or indirectly through the attitudes of the white or Hispanic residents. A second potential explanation for this divergence of the black coefficient from that of whites and Hispanics is that black families, particularly female headed households, are more likely to live in rental housing due to low incomes, thus diluting the segregation of non-family black households from black family households.

The second life cycle variable included in the model captures the preferences of family households to cluster in proximity with other families with children. The pattern of coefficients for the variable FAMWC provides an interesting contrast to the NFAM variable. This variable represents the interaction between the dummy variable for family status of the chooser and the percent of households in a given census tract which are families with children. The coefficients for whites and Hispanics are almost identical, again, with values of 0.022 and 0.021, and t-statistics of 13.5 and 12.3, respectively. The coefficient for blacks is again significantly different than that for whites and Hispanics, but in this case it is substantially higher, with a value of 0.032, and a t-statistic of 16.3. This result may be due to a strong preference by black families to avoid concentrations of non-family blacks in high crime apartment areas.

The third life cycle variable in the model is intended to measure the degree to which elderly households tend to exhibit residential segregation from younger households, either as a result of the natural aging of neighborhoods after families are raised and children leave home, or as a result of residential mobility among the elderly to choose locations which are convenient and provide association with others of the same age. The variable AGE64 is computed as an interaction between the dummy variable for choosers over age 64 and the percent of household heads in each census tract which are over 64 years of age. The coefficients for this variable are 0.020 for blacks, 0.042 for whites, and 0.093 for Hispanics, with t-statistics of 2.4, 7.1, and 7.0, respectively. These results reflect widely divergent patterns of age segregation between whites, blacks, and Hispanics. The low level of age segregation among blacks may be due to the overriding dominance of racial segregation in patterning the residential opportunities for blacks, and the low incomes of elderly blacks, further limiting their residential opportunities to low-income black areas with a wide mix of ages. Whites exhibit a higher degree of age segregation than blacks, and higher than the segregation tendency among whites on the basis of family and non-family status. Hispanics reflect the highest coefficient on this variable, potentially reflecting a substantial differentiation between older long-time residents who are well assimilated into the region residentially and newer immigrants who are more likely to be concentrated in the barrios, or alternatively, the more recent invasion of older Anglo neighborhoods, without a subsequent white flight from the neighborhoods.

Choice of housing tenure

Four variables are included in the model to analyze the housing tenure choice of workers. These are an ownership dummy, and interaction terms for income, age, and family status. Table 5.10 summarizes the tenure distribution among the three population groups in our model.

Table 5.10 Housing tenure

	White	Black	Hispanic
Own	54%	42%	41%
Rent	46%	58%	59%

The variable OWN acts as an intercept for an ownership propensity function of income, age, and family status. The variable therefore represents the base propensity of households to own rather than rent housing, holding constant the influence of income, age, and family status. The coefficients for this variable are -3.75 for whites, -4.32 for blacks, and -4.05 for Hispanics, with t-statistics of -62.1, -68.4, and -66.6, respectively. The coefficients would be expected to be negative when the function is evaluated at the base income, young age, and non-family household status as is the case here. The fact that the coefficient is less negative for whites than Hispanics, and less negative for Hispanics than blacks does represent an important difference between these groups, however, especially considering that the aggregate probability of owning is slightly higher for blacks than Hispanics. Some of the difference may be attributable to differences in non-income wealth, such as inheritance, investments, or other sources of wealth or 'permanent income', and some may be due to different perceptions of risk in the housing purchase transaction between these groups, with blacks being the most uncertain about their economic future.

The variable INCOWN, or the income interaction with homeownership, is calculated as the interaction of the income of the chooser and the ownership dummy. As expected, the income interaction is positive for all three population groups, consistent with the perception that homeownership is a normal good. The magnitude of the coefficients differ between the groups, however, with a coefficient for whites of 0.000054, for blacks of 0.000045, and for Hispanics of 0.000063, with t-statistics of 26.2, 21.6, and 34.4, respectively. The difference in the coefficient between the three groups may be the result of some combination of stronger cultural preferences among Hispanics for land and homeownership, different attitudes between the three groups towards financial risk, or discrimination among real estate agents and mortgage institutions against blacks.

The age interaction with homeownership, AGEOWN, is an interaction between the ownership dummy and the age of the chooser. The coefficients for this variable are 0.074, 0.082, and 0.065 for whites, blacks, and Hispanics, with t-statistics of 51.7, 59.6, and 45.0, respectively. Positive coefficients on this variable are not unexpected, even when holding income and family status constant. This may reflect changing attitudes towards homeownership as age increases, both in terms of the preference for stability, quiet, and independence of homeownership as compared to rental, and in terms of the willingness to take the financial risks of homeownership. It may also reflect an age gap, in which older households purchased homes at a time when homeownership may have been more affordable, and did not as often require two or more incomes to support mortgage payments.

The influence of family status on tenure choice is estimated by FAMOWN, an interaction term of the ownership dummy with the family status dummy. The coefficients for this variable are 0.77, 0.67, and 0.85 for whites, blacks, and Hispanics, with t-statistics of 21.8, 20.7, and 22.3. The coefficients would clearly be expected to be positive, mirroring the life cycle transition from young singles living in apartments, to married couples with families living in suburban homes. But while the coefficients are all positive, they again vary by group. Hispanics may again be expressing a stronger cultural preference for land and homeownership, perhaps dating to more rural and agricultural roots in Mexico and Latin America. Blacks, on the other hand, are not likely expressing a distaste for homeownership, but rather less opportunity to express their preference for homeownership, not as a result of poverty, which is being controlled for, but more likely as a result of restricted residential opportunities.

Choice of workplace

We turn our attention now to the workplace choice dimension of the model. This group of variables estimate the influence of job supply, wages, location, and race on the choice of workplace, by skill level. The educational distribution of the population at risk of being included in our sample is presented in Table 5.11.

Table 5.11 Educational attainment of workers

	White	Black	Hispanic
Less than 4th Grade	0%	1%	12%
4th-6th Grade	1%	3%	18%
7th-9th Grade	6%	10%	15%
10th-11th Grade	9%	14%	11%
12th Grade	29%	36%	21%
1st Year College	8%	8%	5%
2nd Year College	10%	10%	7%
3rd Year College	5%	4%	3%
4th Year College	17%	7%	4%
More than 5 Yrs	14%	5%	5%

Of note in this profile of educational attainment is the dramatically higher proportion of whites with four or more years of college than either blacks or

Hispanics, and the dramatically higher proportion of Hispanics which did not complete High School, compared to either blacks or whites. These educational disparities obviously condition the occupational choices available to each group, and the subsequent opportunities for socioeconomic advancement.

Job Supply Job supply, controlling for journey to work travel time, wages, and occupation or skill level, would have to be considered an overriding influence on an individual's choice of workplace, since the size of the job supply at each location dictates the opportunities for employment there. The model results confirm the importance of job supply, but vary significantly across race and skill levels. Taking low skilled jobs and workers first, the variable ED1SHR is the interaction between the dummy for low skilled workers and the share of the regional total of low skilled jobs which are located in each census tract. The variables ED2SHR, ED3SHR, and ED4SHR represent identically defined interaction terms for low skilled, skilled, and high skilled jobs, respectively. The skill levels are defined as less than high school education, high school, one to four years of college, and more than four years of college.

Figure 5.3 summarizes the coefficients for these variables, for whites, blacks, and Hispanics. The values of the coefficients are shown above each bar. The most immediately apparent pattern in this group of coefficients is that the magnitude of the coefficients for the high skill category is much higher than the other skill levels, for all three groups. This pattern is consistent with an increased geographic clustering of high skilled jobs in the office centers of the metropolitan area, such as the central business districts and suburban office parks, as well as in major defense contractors in the area. If the high skilled jobs are tightly clustered geographically, then the size of the high skilled job base in each census tract is likely to become a more dominant influence on the choice of workplace for high skilled workers.

A second pattern evident in these coefficients is that the peak for high skilled jobs is higher for Hispanics than for whites, and is much higher for blacks than for either of the other two groups. Following the reasoning above, this would indicate that the employment opportunities for high skilled Hispanics are more restricted to large employment centers, and high skilled blacks are even more restricted in their choice of workplace to large high skilled employment centers, such as the central business districts. The results may also obtain from the very low proportions of black and hispanic workers which fall into the high educational category, perhaps increasing the sensitivity to high skill job supply.

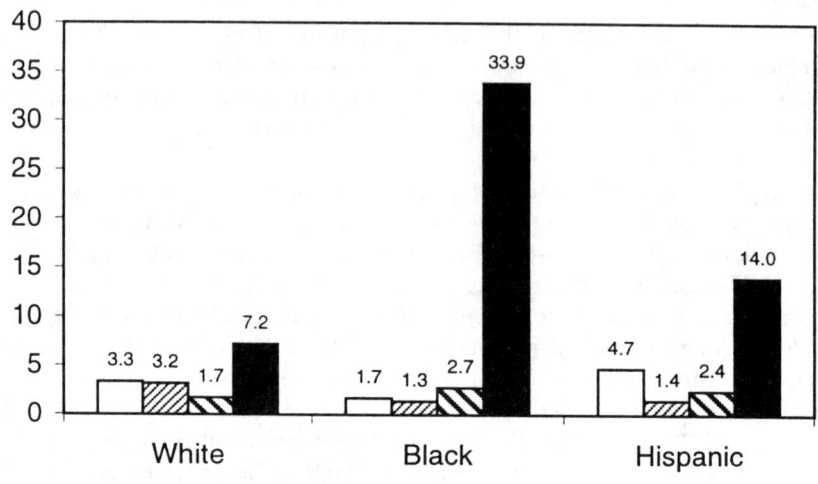

☐ED1SHR ▨ED2SHR ◪ED3SHR ■ED4SHR

Figure 5.3 Coefficients on job supply variables, by race

Workplace Suburbanization The variables DALCBDW, DALCBDW2, FWCBDW, FWCBDW2 represent the travel time from the workplace location to the respective CBD's, and are intended to capture the degree of decentralization of employment opportunities. Figures 5.4 and 5.5 show the travel time functions for these two CBD's.

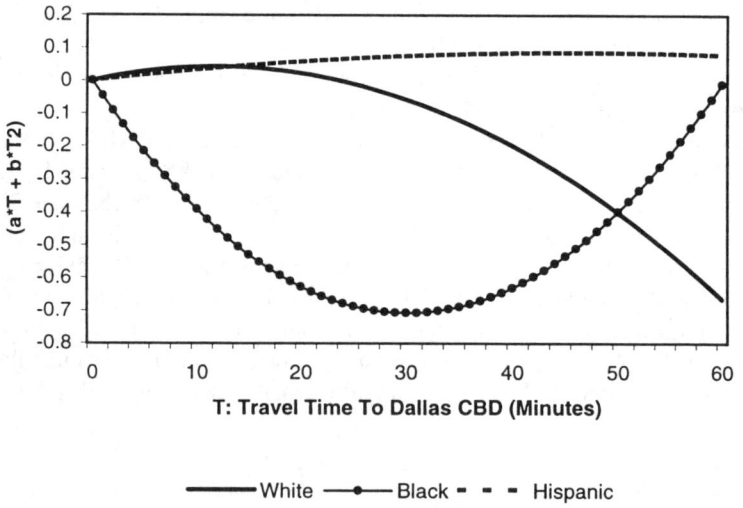

Figure 5.4 Travel time function from workplace to Dallas CBD

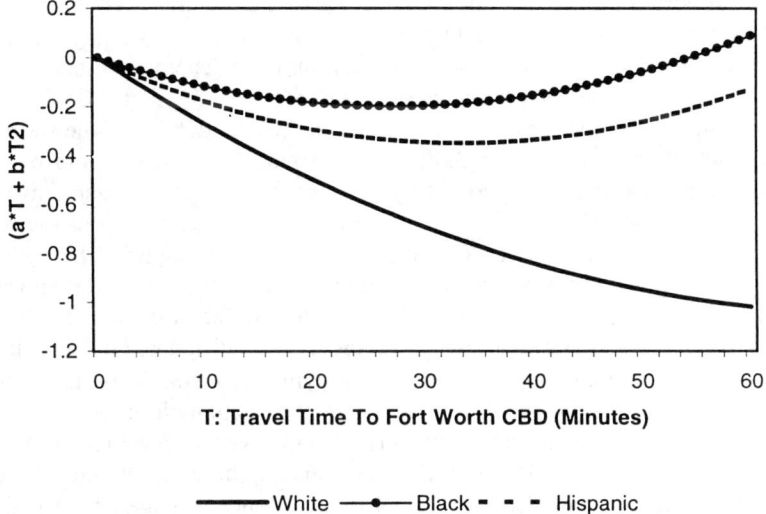

Figure 5.5 Travel time function from workplace to Ft. Worth CBD

We observe from these graphs that the effect of the workplace decentralization variables is much smaller than that of residential decentralization, within the range of reasonable commuting distance. These variables, of course, represent only a partial effect, since we control for several correlated factors such as residential decentralization, population and employment density, and travel time from home to work. The fact that the influence of this function is significantly less than that of residential decentralization may reflect the balancing of the large central employment concentrations by emerging suburban employment centers.

An unusual pattern emerges in comparing the workplace suburbanization function for the two counties. The function declines rapidly for blacks with respect to the Dallas CBD, then rises at increasing distance, reaching zero at approximately 60 minutes from the Dallas CBD. Whites show a slow declining function with respect to the Dallas CBD, and Hispanics reveal a virtually flat function as distance to the Dallas CBD increases. The u-shaped function of blacks may represent the restriction of employment opportunities to the central employment area, possibly because of employment discrimination, or as an indirect result of their residential segregation. It is likely that the increase in the function at large distances is an artifact of the exponential function used, and bears little significance, since there are few black jobs in remote sections of the study area.

In Tarrant County, all three population groups show a u-shaped function, though very flat, with the function for whites lying somewhat below those of blacks and Hispanics. The shape of these functions may be due to the relatively small proportion of the metropolitan jobs located in central Fort Worth, and the pull of more decentralized employment locations in Tarrant County, particularly large manufacturers such as General Dynamics, General Motors, and Bell Helicopter, all located at significant distance from the Fort Worth CBD.

In comparing the results of both the residential and the workplace suburbanization functions for Dallas and Tarrant Counties, it would be well to compare the historical evolution of these two central cities and their surrounding suburbs. Fort Worth emerged as a cattle town, as the beginning of the west, as Dallas established itself as a regional financial and trade center. These historical paths have given the two cities a distinctly different flavor, which we must assume affects the ecology of location within the two central counties. The most obvious difference between the counties is the difference in the level of development, particularly in terms of employment. Dallas grew faster than its neighbor to the west as the sectors in which it had strength grew rapidly on the national scale, eventually leading to the current level of development in Dallas county reaching the edges of the county and spilling north into Collin and Denton Counties, while the growth in Tarrant County remained more residential in character, and tended to fill in the mid-cities area - the suburbs situated between Dallas and Fort Worth. The employment base in Tarrant County remains oriented more to manufacturing than Dallas, which has developed a strong base of electronics and telecommunications to augment its historical strength in finance and trade.

An assessment of employment density gradients will further clarify the differences between the two counties, and the actual level of employment suburbanization which has ocurred in the metropolitan area. Density gradients were calculated in the same way as the residential density gradients, in terms of jobs per acre. The results are reported in Table 5.12.

Table 5.12 Employment density gradients

Geographic Scope	Total	White	Black	Hispanic
2-County	-.197*	-.173*	-.343*	-.258*
Dallas County	-.216*	-.188*	-.375*	-.289*
Tarrant County	-.170*	-.153*	-.301*	-.222*
	Unskilled	Low Skilled	Skilled	High Skilled
2-County	-.189*	-.169*	-.176*	-.165*
Dallas County	-.205*	-.193*	-.209*	-.185*
Tarrant County	-.166*	-.134*	-.129*	-.140*

* Significant at the 5 percent level

These density gradients clarify that white employment opportunities are much more dispersed throughout the metropolitan area than either blacks or Hispanics, and that Hispanic employment opportunities are more dispersed than those of blacks. Tarrant County has a consistently flatter employment density gradient than Dallas county, most probably due to the smaller CBD in Fort Worth, and the rise of significant suburban employment in the D-FW airport, and the suburbs between Dallas and Fort Worth. The density gradients are fairly consistent across the skill levels of jobs, with low skill jobs tending to have a slightly steeper density gradient.

Wages The variables WAGE1-WAGE4 reflect the mean hourly wage by skill level for each workplace. Holding travel time and skill level constant, wages would be expected to be a dominant influence on workplace choice. Figure 5.6 charts the wage coefficients for each skill level and all three population groups. The coefficients on the wage variables are almost all positive, as expected, but show large differences within and between population groups.

First, we examine the within race pattern of the coefficients. The wage coefficients for all three population groups are higher for the low skilled and skilled jobs than for the unskilled and high skilled jobs. Low skilled jobs have the highest coefficients in all three groups. One plausible interpretation for the pattern of higher coefficients among low skilled and skilled workers, which represent high school graduates and workers with one to four years of college, is that these educational levels, being in the middle of the job skill mix, are the most occupationally fluid, and therefore in a better position to improve their wages by changing workplace, job, or even occupation. The high skilled jobs may be less occupationally fluid because of higher levels of specialization: one does not often abandon a medical school education to become a lawyer. Unskilled workers, on the other hand, may be less effective in the job search process, and may have less resources with which to conduct the job search, thus allowing them less efficiency in choosing workplaces which optimize their wages, ceteris paribus.

The differences in wage coefficients between races are in some cases quite substantial. The unskilled wage coefficients are much lower for Hispanics than whites, and are almost zero for blacks. This result may be consistent with the argument posited above, that the lowest skilled workers have less resources and abilities to conduct an optimal job search. The disparity between whites and Hispanics and blacks within the same skill category, however, suggests that blacks and Hispanics are at a disadvantage in competing for the higher wage unskilled jobs, either because of their relative inaccessibility given their residential constraints, or because employers differentiate between these groups in their hiring and pay practices, or both.

The racial pattern is the most pronounced in the high skill category, where the coefficient for Hispanics is indistinguishable from zero, and the coefficient for blacks is significantly negative. It would be unrealistic to ascribe a negative wage coefficient among high skilled blacks to a lack of job search capabilities, or resources. One would be hard pressed to postulate an explanation which would attribute a negative wage coefficient to the preferences of workers - that would be equivalent to arguing that income is an economic bad.

In the two middle skill categories, the wage coefficients for whites and Hispanics are similar, if somewhat lower for Hispanics. But the coefficients for blacks are significantly higher than both whites and Hispanics in the low skilled and skilled job categories. This may reflect more open hiring practices in mid-skilled jobs such as government jobs in the central business district.

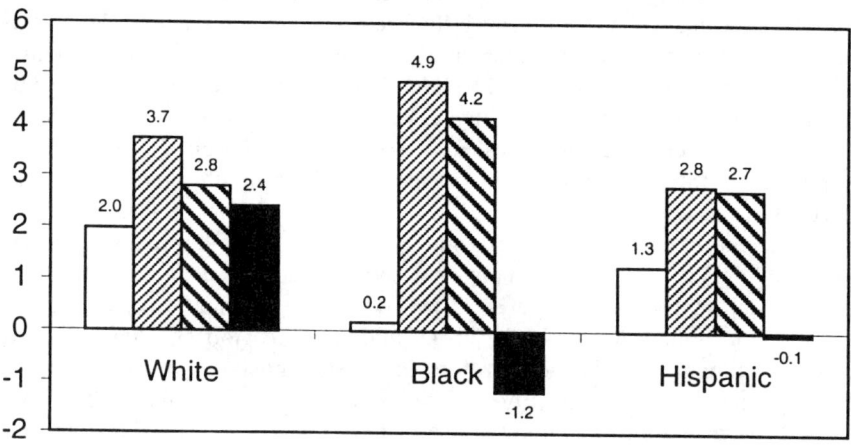

Figure 5.6 Coefficients on wage variables, by race

Wage gradients by skill level and race were calculated to shed additional light on the interpretation of these wage effects, and are summarized in Table 5.13.

These wage gradients reveal a negative wage gradient for whites at all skill levels, indicating that whites, which are widely suburbanized in their residential location, require higher wages to accept jobs at the center of the city, with high parking and congestion costs. Unskilled and low skilled Blacks, on the other hand, face positive wage gradient from the CBD. Skilled blacks have an insignificant positive wage gradient, and high skilled blacks have an insignificant negative gradient. Hispanics reveal insignificant positive wage gradients in all categories, with significant coefficients only in the low skilled category.

Table 5.13 Wage gradients with respect to distance from the CBD

Geographic Scope	Unskilled	Low Skilled	Skilled	High Skilled
White				
2-County	-.0106*	-.0044*	-.0070*	-.0085*
Dallas County	-.0166*	-.0083*	-.0097*	-.0131*
Tarrant County	-.0027	.0004	-.0035	-.0026
Black				
2-County	.0132*	.0142*	.0022	-.0035
Dallas County	.0158*	.0153*	.0020	-.0102
Tarrant County	.0045	.0106	.0035	.0185
Hispanic				
2-County	.0045	.0132*	.0032	.0122
Dallas County	.0060	.0045	.0064	.0070
Tarrant County	.0020	.0265*	-.0022	-.0139

* Significant at the 5 percent level

Straszheim (1980) found positive wage gradients from the ghetto for unskilled blacks, and negative wage gradients, approximating those of whites, for higher skilled workers. Our results parallel Straszheim's positive wage gradient from the ghetto for the lowest skilled blacks, and at higher levels, a wage gradient for blacks approaching the negative wage gradient for whites. Strazheim interpreted these findings as evidence supporting Kain's (1968) claim that the restriction of residential location of low skilled blacks through residential segregation creates a spatially differentiated labor market with excess supply of labor in the ghetto, driving down wages for unskilled or low skilled jobs there. Suburbanization of higher skill blacks, according to Strazheim, leads to a wage gradient more similar to that of whites.

While our wage gradient results follow those of Strazheim, both his results and ours reveal a large disparity in wages between whites, blacks, and Hispanics at the city center, which diminishes as distance from the CBD increases for reference, our wage gradient results are graphed in Appendix C). If black residential segregation creates excess labor supply for unskilled jobs at the city center, and this spatial imbalance drives down black wages at the city center, as Strazheim argues, why then are wages for whites in unskilled jobs at the city center significanty higher than black or Hispanic wages for the same unskilled jobs? If employers differentiate between employees on the basis of education or skill level, and not on the basis of race, then excess unskilled labor at the city center should drive the wages of all unskilled workers down to similar levels, regardless of race.

Although the spatial imbalance caused by black residential concentration in the city center should be expected to increase competition for a limited supply of jobs, this explanation alone is insufficient for the earnings disparity between whites, blacks, and Hispanics. The following table demonstrates the magnitude of the earnings gap for workers of the same educational level, suggesting unequal treatment of workers of similar educational background, on the basis of race or ethnicity.

Table 5.14 Mean annual wages by educational attainment (1979$)

	White	Black	Hispanic
Less than 4th Grade	$11,500	$ 7,500	$ 7,600
4th-6th Grade	$11,500	$ 7,300	$ 9,000
7th-9th Grade	$11,900	$ 8,700	$ 9,800
10th-11th Grade	$12,700	$ 8,500	$10,200
12th Grade	$14,000	$ 9,800	$12,300
1st Year College	$14,400	$10,400	$14,900
2nd Year College	$16,000	$10,900	$13,900
3rd Year College	$17,200	$11,400	$13,000
4th Year College	$23,000	$13,700	$16,200
More than 5 Yrs	$23,800	$15,000	$17,700
All	$17,000	$10,100	$11,200

Workplace Racial Segregation The next set of variables (PCTBLK1-PCTBLK4) describes the influence on workplace choice of the percent of the jobs which are held by blacks, by skill level, at each workplace. This set of variables is intended to capture the preferences for racial segregation in the workplace, after accounting for skill levels, job supply, wages, and workplace accessibility. The pattern of these coefficients is shown in figure 5.7.

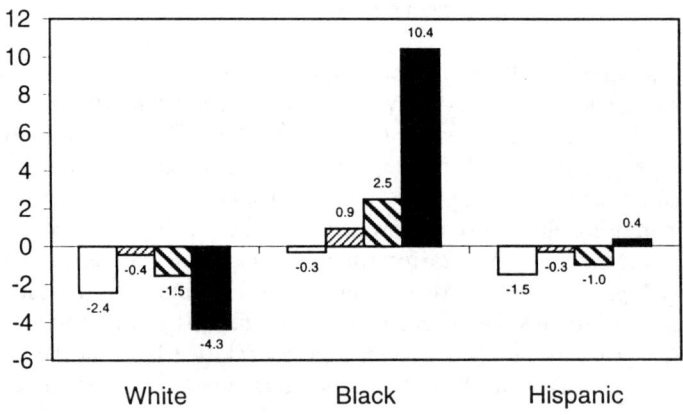

Figure 5.7 Coefficients on workplace percent black

104

Not surprisingly, these effects are strong. Among whites, these variables have significant negative coefficients for all four skill levels. The tendency for workplace segregation is pronounced among unskilled workers, decreases among low skilled workers (those with a high school education), and then increases among skilled workers, and becomes the most pronounced among high skilled white workers. Although one might expect that as educational levels increase, racial prejudice would decrease, the most direct interpretation of these coefficients would tend to refute that expectation. The lower magnitude of the negative coefficients for low skilled and skilled jobs, those in the middle of the job spectrum, may be due to a greater mobility and mix of these jobs throughout the metropolitan area: such jobs as construction and food service, which would tend to reduce the level of segregation in these jobs. This interpretation would be consistent with the finding that these two job categories were the same ones for which blacks showed exceptionally high coefficients on the wage variables.

It is possible that the relatively strong negative coefficient for unskilled whites is due to a combination of stronger held prejudices at low socioeconomic levels where status competition is likely to be the strongest between races, and to a tendency for unskilled workers to work close to their residential locations due to their lower ability to overcome search and transportation costs for more distant jobs.

The coefficients on the percent black in the workplace are lower in magnitude for Hispanics than for whites, but are for the most part still negative. The largest coefficient is for unskilled jobs, and the next largest is for skilled jobs. Low skilled and high skilled jobs have insignificant negative and positive coefficients, respectively. The insignificant negative coefficient for low skilled jobs may follow the same reasoning applied earlier to the coefficients for whites, which had the smallest coefficient on this skill level: jobs requiring a high school education are perhaps the most likely to be highly mixed in the workplace, due to the interchangeability of workers and jobs. For high skilled workers, however, which represent the most highly specialized jobs, an insignificant positive coefficient may imply that Hispanics are finding employment opportunities opened by affirmative action in the same places that high skilled blacks are.

The coefficients on percent black in the workplace reveal a consistent, and dramatic, pattern across skill levels. The coefficients increase from an insignificant negative coefficient for unskilled jobs to a value of 2.5 for skilled jobs, and 10.5 for high skilled jobs. The strong, consistent increase with increasing educational and skill levels would appear to contradict the expectation that at higher education and status levels, blacks are more likely to prefer to integrate into the mainstream, white, economy and workplace. But this pattern may be more consistent with a pattern of increasing job discrimination at progressively higher skill and status levels. If it has been clearly demonstrated that whites tend to avoid minorities, especially blacks, in residential location as their incomes increase, it should not be surprising that whites express these same prejudices in the workplace through a combination of the aggregation of the workplace choices of individual white workers, and discriminatory hiring practices of predominantly white businesses.

The group of variables describing the percent of the jobs held by Hispanics (PCTSPN1-PCTSPN4) provide an interesting contrast to the percent black worker variables, and are summarized in figure 5.8. The pattern of coefficients for whites is significantly different than on percent black. The lowest three skill levels have positive coefficients, but the high skilled job category registered a strong negative coefficient of -3.2. It appears, first, that whites do not have as strong a negative reaction to Hispanics in the workplace as seems to exist against blacks. The negative coefficient on high skilled jobs may be due to the correlation between high proportions of Hispanic and black high skilled workers in the workplace, possibly in government and defense industry locations strongly influenced by affirmative action programs. This result could also obtain from an underlying preference for segregation not only residentially, but also in the workplace, which can be more effectively realized by members of all three groups at higher skill (and wage) levels.

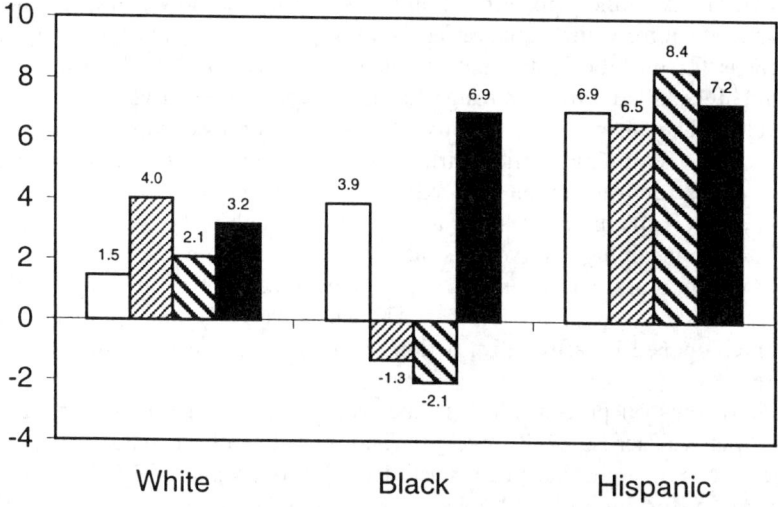

□ PCTSPN1 ▨ PCTSPN2 ◪ PCTSPN3 ■ PCTSPN4
Figure 5.8 Coefficients on workplace percent hispanic

The reaction of blacks to the percent of the workers in the workplace who are Hispanic appears to be positive for the extremes of unskilled and high skilled jobs, but negative for low skilled and skilled jobs. The positive coefficient on high skilled jobs is consistent with the preceding argument that high skilled blacks and Hispanics appear to have made some headway in gaining entry into the job market in certain locations which may be more responsive to affirmative action hiring regulations, although at lower wages, as noted in the discussion of the variable WAGE4 earlier. The positive coefficient for unskilled jobs may be a reflection of the residential proximity of unskilled blacks and Hispanics to industrial areas, where they compete for the same jobs. A preference for workplaces with low numbers of Hispanic workers prevails within low skilled and skilled blacks.

The pattern of coefficients for Hispanics on the percent Hispanic worker variables shows a consistently high positive pattern, varying from 6.5 to 8.4. This pattern reflects a fairly consistent level of ethnic solidarity in the workplace among Hispanics.

The journey to work

The relationship between residence and workplace is defined by the journey to work, estimated in this model as a quadratic function of the travel time in minutes, from residence census tract to workplace census tract. If we evaluate the quadratic function of travel time using the estimated coefficients on TIME and TIME2 from the model, we obtain a disutility of travel function common to transportation planning models. The general shape of this disutility of travel function will be a critical variable in determining the shape and density of an urban area. The travel disutility function for each of the three population groups is plotted in figure 5.9.

The travel disutility functions of whites and Hispanics are virtually identical, with both showing a typical decay function in which the rate of decay decreases as travel time increases. The function for blacks, however, shows an almost linear decay function, decreasing at a slightly increasing rate as the travel time increases. The decay function of blacks lies slightly above that of whites and Hispanics within the normal commute radius, and crosses the decay function of whites and Hispanics between 50 and 60 minutes of travel time. This result implies that within the normal range of commuting, blacks have to travel slightly farther than whites or Hispanics, but are less likely to make the extremely long commute often associated with wealthy suburban or exurban households.

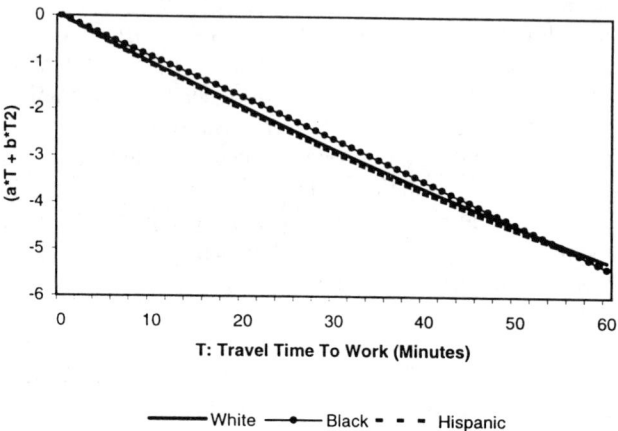

Figure 5.9 Disutility of travel in the journey to work

These results can be checked against average travel time distributions by income, presented in Table 5.15.

Table 5.15 Mean travel time to work by income

Family Income (1979 $)	White	Black	Hispanic
Under $10,000	20	23	21
$10-20,000	23	25	22
$20,000-30,000	24	24	23
$30,000-40,000	24	26	23
$40,000-50,000	24	26	26
$50,000 or More	21	24	20
All Workers	21	24	22

In reviewing the results presented in Table 5.15, recall that our sample does not include transit passengers. Although transit usage in the Dallas-Fort Worth area is very low - less than 2 percent of the total commuting trips, these transit trips are heavily concentrated among 'transit captives' - those without other means of transportation. These transit captives are predominantly low income blacks and Hispanics who do not own an automobile. This omission will tend to underrepresent the travel time for blacks and Hispanics with the lowest incomes, since transit travel times are considerably longer than auto travel times. Table 5.15 does reveal, however, a 14% higher average travel time to work for blacks compared to whites, with the highest differences at both the low and high ends of the income distribution. The average travel time of Hispanics is only slightly higher than whites, on average.

6 Conclusions and directions for future research

Conclusions

The shape and texture of metropolitan development results from a complex interaction between firms supplying jobs, landowners supplying land, developers supplying housing and commercial space, households making an array of choices, including workplace, housing tenure, and residence location, and government regulating these interactions. This study explores only one portion of this complex dynamic, the dimensions of household choice, holding the other components constant. The analysis is partial equilibrium and static, representing a snapshot of only one point in time, and one urban area. Despite these limitations, the analysis does shed some light on the complexities and interrelationships between the three dimensions of household choice analyzed here.

The derivation and use of a multinomial logit model of residence, tenure, and workplace holds promise for integrating the most productive elements from several separate streams of research bearing on the urban spatial structure, including gravity models, monocentric models, and models of social ecology. The model developed here is consistent with neoclassical urban economics and random utility theory, but goes beyond the monocentric model and the gravity model in the behavioral content of household choices by incorporating elements from social and urban ecology.

Relation to primary theoretical traditions

In the following sections, we review the relationship of our model results to the principal theoretical traditions from which the current approach has drawn, and the implications of our research in light of these theoretical traditions.

The gravity model Although the Gravity model has received perhaps the most widespread application in land use and transportation modeling and planning, and is in general use currently in many major metropolitan planning agencies, its lack of a rigorous theoretical and behavioral foundation has led to much ongoing criticism. Disaggregation of household types by income quartile has been implemented in certain of these models, but disaggregation of household characteristics has rarely extended beyond this level. The gravity models in current planning use, such as the DRAM and EMPAL models developed and supported by Putman (1983), typically are separated into an employment allocation model, and a residential allocation model, which are run sequentially. The general assumption is that employment location is largely driven by lagged employment location and current accessibility to lagged residential location, and that residential location is largely based on current employment location.

While this class of models does not explicitly assume a monocentric urban form, it does assume a particular choice sequence, with employment location followed by residential location, consistent with economic base theory. The ability to explore the interdependence between residential location and employment location decisions without an assumed structure of the choice structure has not been incorporated into any of the gravity models in current use, to the author's knowledge.

Our findings suggest that the locational calculus of persons of different race, ethnicity, socioeconomic status, and stage of life cycle are significantly different, and need to be incorporated into models of residential location. The gravity model framework can be extended to incorporate further household type disaggregation, but the calibration procedures in current use have difficulty in identifying the standard errors and significance of individual independent variables, rendering them less effective for exploratory research.

The model developed here closely parallels the structure of a doubly constrained gravity model, resolves some of the estimation problems, adds a grounding in urban economic theory and random utility theory, and incorporates some of the behavioral richness of social ecological theory. This framework may lend itself in the future to use as both a research technique and a strategic planning tool.

The monocentric model The monocentric model has been used widely as an analytical tool, if not a practical planning tool, due to its rigorous (and restrictive) assumptions. The assumption that all employment is located at the city center is clearly unrealistic in the face of massive suburbanization not only of households, but of businesses. Suburban office parks are an integral part of the modern urban landscape. In the case of a metropolitan area which grew together from two historically distinct and geographically separate central cities, as has occurred in the Dallas-Fort Worth area, the concept of monocentricity has little meaning.

Some attempts have been made to extend the monocentric model to reflect decentralized employment location, but the calculus of the monocentric model dictates that decentralization be expressed in only one dimension: distance from the CBD. Two problems exist with this approach. First, is does not realistically reflect the effect of suburban employment centers, much less a second CBD, on the employment density surface of the urban area. The standard density gradient does not fit well the case of a declining density gradient from the CBD to a suburban employment ring, at which point density peaks, and subsequently declines again. Second, the nature of the monocentric model is a one dimensional representation of location within an urban area. This limitation has been acknowledged by Mills (1973), but keeps the mathematics tractable and allows some useful analytical results to be derived from the model.

The main problem with a one dimensional representation of location within the metropolitan area is that this implies a symmetrical distribution of activity with respect to the CBD. Almost any urban area will in reality have elements of concentric rings of development differentiated by age of development, stage of life cycle, or status, as well as sectors or wedges differentiated by status, and pockets of ethnic or racial segregation. A one dimensional, symmetrical representation of an urban area is inherently incapable of capturing this web-like texture.

Siegel (1975) and Simpson (1980, 1987) have attempted to extend the monocentric model to allow workplace choice to be modeled jointly with residence choice. The fundamental difficulty with their approach, however, lies in the calculus of the monocentric model, which treats all locations one dimensionally: distance from the CBD. The relationship between residential and workplace location cannot therefore be explicitly captured within the monocentric model framework, since both are measured with respect to the CBD, and not with respect to each other. If both are 5 miles from the CBD, but the residence is north of the CBD and the workplace is south, the actual commute is 10 miles, and the model assumes it to be zero.

Discrete choice theory The development of the theory of random utility, and its applications to problems of discrete choice, provide a solid framework on which to develop models of household behavior. Whereas the models of urban economics are based on consumer economic theory with the assumption that consumers purchase bundles of goods and services which can be measured as continuous nonnegative quantities, the models based on discrete choice theory deal with problems in which the choices can be structured as discrete alternatives. After the early development of the theory in the field of psychology by Luce and Suppes (1965), and the adaptation of the theory to individual choice of travel mode in the transportation planning field by McFadden (1973), discrete choice theory, and the multinomial and nested logit models derived from it have been applied to such problems as residential location, travel mode, and housing tenure by a variety of researchers. The choice of location lends itself to modeling within a discrete choice framework, since a household does not choose how much of a location to use for building a house, but simply which location to choose from the available alternatives.

Anas (1981) has reconciled the multinomial logit model with the gravity model, showing that a doubly constrained gravity model is virtually identical in structure and result to a multinomial logit model of the joint choice of residence and workplace. Anas (1987) has also modeled the monocentric city using multinomial logit, allowing for the presence of random taste variation in an otherwise homogeneous population, and has demonstrated how the random utility framework extends the monocentric model of urban economic theory.

In our research, we find that the multinomial logit specification, based on discrete choice theory, and ultimately, on consumer economic theory, is a useful approach to overcoming many of the inherent limitations identified both in the gravity models and in the monocentric model. The use of this approach allows us to work directly with a household utility function, rather than working with derived demand functions, and therefore allows us flexibility to incorporate variables and hypotheses regarding the influences on households' choices of residence, workplace, and tenure, which are drawn from the domain of social ecology as well as urban economics.

Beyond the assumption of exogenous workplace   Perhaps the most compelling of the findings of this study are that that assumption of exogenous workplace endemic in each of the streams of modeling literature referenced here is inconsistent with empirical evidence. Our tests of choice model structures consistent with the exogenous workplace assumption consistently failed statistical tests, and reduced to joint choice specifications. While we recognize that not all residence and workplace decisions are made simultaneously, the complexity of household circumstances, even for single-worker households most likely to conform to this model, require less restrictive assumptions to be made. This point is further elaborated elsewhere (Waddell, 1993).

In addition, the increasing prevalence of multiple-worker households raises other complications for urban modeling based on the common assumption of single-worker households. These households are even less amenable to the assumption of exogenous workplace, since they must balance more than one commute and job choice against the residential location choice.

Social ecology   Our findings clearly support the conclusions Berry (1983), Berry and Kasarda (1985), and others in the literature of urban and social ecology that there are three dominant factors differentiating population in urban space: status attainment, race and ethnicity, and stage of life cycle. The model developed here, however, goes a step farther to incorporate tenure choice and workplace choice into the same model, allowing for an unusually well integrated view of the urban ecology of one metropolitan area, within a rigorous quantitative framework grounded in discrete choice theory.

There exists the interpretation that 'birds of a feather flock together', that wealthy whites prefer to live with other wealthy whites, families with other families, Hispanics with other Hispanics, blacks with other blacks. The evidence is clear that race, ethnicity, stage of life cycle, and socioeconomic status are salient dimensions of spatial residential clustering. The difficult question to resolve is: to what extent is it a positive association of persons with similar tastes and lifestyles choosing to reside in close proximity, and to what extent is it a matter of exclusion or avoidance? While our results cannot definitively address this question, there is substantial evidence that both mechanisms are involved.

Perhaps the most dominant pattern in the results of this analysis is the degree to which race influences the urban social ecology, by segregating not only residential neighborhoods, but to a significant extent, workplaces. And though the evidence of ethnic prejudice appears to impact the Hispanic community, the effect seems much more pernicious for blacks. Not only are blacks avoided by both whites and Hispanics in residence and workplace, but wages are lower for blacks at each skill level. The compounding of racial avoidance in both the residence and the workplace appears to further isolate blacks, leading to continued abandonment of the black ghettoes to the poorest blacks. A critical question is whether these poorest blacks are unable to leave the core of the ghetto to assimilate into the white mainstream due to unemployment and poverty, or whether poor blacks remain in the ghetto because of a rejection of white mainstream society and values, and the adoption of an alternative value structure which accepts crime, violence, drugs, broken homes, teenage pregnancy, educational failure, and unemployment as inevitable. Our study scope cannot begin to address the issues surrounding the culture of poverty.

Instead, within this study, we have focused not on the poorest strata of the population, but on those fully employed and participating in the mainstream economy.

Our results indicate that blacks have a desire to assimilate into mainstream, white society through residential propinquity. Higher incomes and lower ages seem to allow blacks to more effectively translate these desires for socioeconomic mobility into spatial assimilation than poorer and older blacks. In spite of these assimilation preferences, however, areas near high concentrations of blacks seen to face an almost inevitable flight of white population, and an associated decline of housing value, while large percent increases in black population in white areas geographically remote from the ghetto did not precipitate any such reaction.

Our results can largely be seen as supporting those of Berry's (1976) study of the Chicago housing market from 1968-1972, which provided evidence to support the thesis that during periods of rapid housing construction, the normal pace of housing filtering accelerates rapidly. As a result of rapid movement of whites to the peripheral housing development and the rapid movement of blacks from the interior of the ghetto into adjacent areas being vacated by whites, the ghetto is left with increasing levels of abandoned housing, and the price of housing for blacks declines. To quote from Berry's (1976) conclusions:

1. It is appropriate, indeed necessary, in housing market studies to recognize that the metropolis is a spatially arrayed stratification system, with relatively homogeneous neighborhood submarkets differentiated by income levels and socioeconomic status, race, and ethnic affiliation, and age and the residents' stage in the life cycle.

2. These submarkets are linked by filtering mechanisms that have their origin in new construction at the edge of the metropolitan area. When new construction proceeds at a rate exceeding the rate of growth of demand, downward pressure will be exerted upon housing prices in successively older neighborhoods, and neighborhood succession will take place as social groups filter up the scale of housing age and quality. Downward pressure on prices are reflected in differential rates of price increase-highest in the newest and most desirable areas, and lowest in the least desirable neighborhoods where a growing housing surplus produces abandonment-and only later in differences in price levels, when level is controlled for property characteristics and income levels.

Our results tend also to support Massey's (1984) findings that Hispanics are better able than blacks to translate socioeconomic gains into spatial assimilation, once language and acculturation barriers are overcome. Lack of education appears to explain a larger proportion of the socioeconomic gap between Hispanics and whites than between blacks and whites.

Integration of results

What our results add to the body of urban economic and social ecological theory is a more effective identification of the roles of workplace accessibility, residential clustering along the lines of socioeconomic status, stage of life cycle, and race and ethnicity in household choices of residential location, and a more integrated view of the interdependent household choices of residence, workplace, and housing tenure. The methodology provides a bridge between urban economics and social ecology, and permits the exploration of a rich set of questions which overlap disciplinary boundaries.

Directions for future research

Where, then, from here? The major limitations of this research were noted earlier: the analysis is partial equilibrium and static, using data only from 1980; the data is restricted to single earner family households and workers in non-family households who own an automobile and commute to work by car, so the results cannot be extrapolated to multiple-worker families, or the extremely poor, the transit captives.

Related research on multiple-worker households by the author have begun to explore the implications of more than one workplace decision and commute balanced against a household residential location choice (Waddell, 1996). The lack of congruity between decision makers choosing workplace and residential location raises complexities not present in the single-worker case. Addressing this issue will require either disconnecting the residence and workplace choices, or developing a more sophisticated household-individual choice model that allows individual choices to be integrated into a larger household choice models. The tractability of this approach remains to be seen. This related work also takes a dynamic approach to addressing residential mobility and location choices as linked sequential decisions leading to dynamic behavior over time.

The use of discrete choice theory helps to bridge the gap between the disciplines of economics, sociology, and geography, enriching the theoretical content of the field of development studies. Further integration of these disciplines should provide a fertile area for research on urban and regional development in the future. The spatial context provides a common thread for the integration of economic and sociological theory in the study of the development process.

The processes of firm location, and land, commercial and residential development all lend themselves to the spatial discrete choice modeling approach which has been used in this study. Related work by the author and others has applied the discrete choice modeling framework to business location choices (Waddell and Shukla, 1993a, 1993b; Shukla and Waddell, 1991). Further development will be directed towards the integration of household, business, and developer choice models into an integrated urban land use and transportation model, building on a growing and cohesive body of empirical and theoretical research in these areas.

Bibliography

Alonso, William. Location and Land Use. Cambridge: Harvard University Press, 1964.
Anas, Alex. "The Impact of Transit Investment on Housing Values: A Simulation Experiment." Environment and Planning A 11 (1979): 239-255.
Anas, Alex. "A Probabilistic Approach to the Structure of Rental Housing Markets." Journal of Urban Economics 7 (1980): 225-247.
Anas, Alex. "The Estimation of Multinomial Logit Models of Joint Location and Travel Choice from Aggregated Data." Journal of Regional Science 21(2) (1981·): 223-242.
Anas, Alex. Residential Location Markets and Transportation; Economic Theory, Econometrics, and Policy Analysis with Discrete Choice Models. New York: Academic Press, 1982.
Anas, Alex. "Discrete Choice Theory, Information Theory and Multinomial Logit and Gravity Models." Transportation Research Board 17B (1983): 13-23.
Anas, Alex. "Taste Heterogeneity and Urban Spatial Structure: The Logit Model and Monocentric Theory Reconciled." Northwestern University, 1987.
Anas, Alex and G.Y. Lee. "The Potential for a Value Capture Policy to Finance Rapid Transit Projects in Chicago's Southwest Corridor: An Empirical Simulation Analysis." In Research in Urban Economics, ed. J.V. Henderson, 1982.
Anas, Alex. "The Chicago Area Transportation - Land Use Analysis System." Urban and Regional Planning Program, Department of Civil Engineering, Northwestern University, 1983.
Anderson, R.J. and T. Crocker. "Air Pollution and Property Values: A Reply," Review of Economics and Statistics 54 (1972): 470-473.

Apgar, William C., Jr. Applications of Annual Housing Survey Data in Local Policy Planning. Report to U.S. Department of Housing and Urban Development, 1980.

Apgar, William C., Jr., and John F. Kain. "Effects of a Housing Allowance on the Pittsburg Housing Market" In John F. Kain, ed. Progress Report on the Development of the NBER Urban Simulation Model and Interim Analyses of Housing Allowances. New York: National Bureau of Economic Analysis, 1974.

Bailey, Martin J. "A Note on the Economics of Residential Zoning and Urban Renewal." Land Economics 35 (1959) 288-292.

Batty, M. "Design and Construction of a Subregional Land Use Model." Socio-Economic Planning Sciences 5 (1971): 97-124.

Batty, M., and S. Mackie. "The Calibration of Gravity, Entropy, and Related Models of Spatial Interaction." Environment and Planning 4 (1972): 205-233.

Becker, Gary. Human Capital: A Theoretical and Empirical Analysis with Special Reference to Education. New York: Columbia University Press, 1964.

Ben-Akiva, Moshe. "Structure of Travel Demand Models". Ph.D. diss. Massachusetts Institute of Technology, 1973.

Ben-Akiva, Moshe, and Stephen S. Lerman. "Disaggregate Travel and Mobility Choice Models and Measures of Accessibility." In D. Hensher and Peter Stopher, eds. Behavioral Travel Demand Modeling. London: Croom Helm, 1979.

Ben-Akiva, Moshe, and Stephen S. Lerman. Discrete Choice Analysis: Theory and Application to Travel Demand. Cambridge: MIT Press, 1987.

Beesley, M., and M. Dalvi. "Spatial Equilibrium and the Journey to Work". Journal of Transport Economics and Policy 8 (1974).

Berry, Brian J.L. "Ghetto Expansion and Single-Family Housing Prices: Chicago, 1968-1972." Journal of Urban Economics 3 (1976): 397-423.

Berry, Brian J.L. Comparative Urbanization: Divergent Paths in the Twentieth Century. New York: St. Matin's Press, 1981.

Berry, Brian, J.L., and D. Dahman. Population Redistribution in the United States in the 1970's. Washington, D.C.: National Academy of Sciences, 1977.

Berry, Brian J.L. and John Kasarda. Contemporary Urban Ecology. New York: MacMillan, 1977.

Brewer, G.D. Politicians, Bureaucrats, and the Consultant: a Critique of Urban Problem Solving. New York: Basic Books, 1973.

Burgess, Ernest W. "The Growth of the City: An Introduction to a Research Project." In Robert Park, Ernest Burgess, and R.D. McKenzie, eds. The City. Chicago, The University of Chicago Press, 1925.

Burnstein, Alan N. "Immigrants and Residential Mobility: The Irish and Germans in Philadelphia, 1850-1880." In Theodore Hershberg, ed. Philadelphia: Work, Space, Family, and Group Experience in the 19th Century. New York: Oxford University Press, 1981.

Chicago Area Transportation Study (CATS). Chicago Area Transportation Study, Vol. II. Data Projections. July, 1960.

Crecine, J.P. TOMM (Time Oriented Metropolitan Model). Pittsburg: Department of City Planning, 1964. CRP Technical Bulletin no. 6.

Cressey, Paul. "Population Succession in Chicago: 1989-1930." The American Journal of Sociology. 44 (1938): 59-69.

Courant, Paul N. "Urban Residential Structure and Racial Prejudice." Institute of Public Policy Studies, University of Michigan, 1974. Discussion Paper no. 62.

Courant, Paul N., and John Yinger. "On Models of Racial Prejudice and Urban Spatial Structure." Journal of Urban Economics 4 (1977): 272-291.

Daganzo, C., and Y. Scheffi. "Multinomial Probit Models with Time Series Data: Unifying State Dependence and Serial Correlation Models." Environment and Planning A 14 (1982): 1377-1388.

Daly, A., and S. Zachary. "Improved Multiple Choice Models." In Identifying and Measuring the Determinants of Mode Choice. D. Hensher and Q. Dalvi, eds. London: Teakfield, 1979.

DeLeeuw, Frank, and Raymond Struyk. The Web of Urban Housing. Washington, D.C.: Urban Land Institute, 1975.

Dixit, A. "The Optimum Factory Town." Bell Journal of Econom. Management Science 4 (1973): 637-651.

Dodd, Stuart C. "The Interacance Hypothesis - A Gravity Model Fitting Physical Masses and Human Groups." American Sociological Review 15 (1950): 245-256.

Domencich, T., and Daniel McFadden. Urban Travel Demand - A Behavioral Analysis. Amsterdam: North Holland, 1975.

Duncan, Otis Dudley, and Beverly Duncan. The Negro Population of Chicago: A Study of Residential Succession. Chicago: University of Chicago Press, 1957.

Ellwood, David T. "The Spatial Mismatch Hypothesis: Are There Teenage Jobs Missing in the Ghetto?" Harvard University and National Bureau of Economic Research, 1983.

Esslinger, Dean R. Immigrants and the City: Ethnicity and Mobility in a 19th Century Midwestern Community. Port Washington, NY: Kennikat, 1975.

Freeman, A.M. III. "On Estimating Air Pollution Control Benifits From Land Value Studies." Journal of Environmental Economics and Management 1 (1974): 74-83.

Fulton, Philip N. "Procedure Used for Allocating Incomplete Place-of-Work Responses in the 1980 Census Urban Transportation Planning Package." Paper presented at the Annual Meeting of the Transportation Research Board, Washington, D.C., 1983.

Garin, R.A. "A Matrix Formulation of the Lowry Model for Intra-metropolitan Activity Location." Journal of the American Institute of Planners 32 (1966): 361-364.

Goldner, William. Projective Land Use Model (PLUM). Berkeley: Bay Area Transportation Study Commission, 1968. BATSC Technical Report 219.

Goldner, William, S.R. Rosenthall, and J.R. Meredith. Projective Land Use Model-PLUM: Theory and Application. Berkeley: Institute of Transportation and Traffic Engineering, University of California, 1972.

Gordon, Ian, and Roger Vickerman. "Opportunity, Preference, and Constraint: An Approach to the Analysis of Metropolitan Migration." Urban Studies 19 (1982): 247-261.

Gordon, M.M. Assimilation in American Life. New York: Oxford University Press, 1964.

Greene, William H. LIMDEP. Chicago, Northwestern University, 1986.

Greenwood, M. "Research on Internal Migration in the United States." Journal of Economic Literature 13 (1975): 397-433.

Guest, A.M., and J.A. Weed. "Ethnic Residential Segregation: Patterns of Change." American Journal of Sociology. 81 (1976): 1088-1111.

Hamilton, Bruce W. "Wasteful Commuting." Journal of Political Economy 90 (1982): 1035-1053.

Hamburg, John. Land Use Forecasts: Chicago. Chicago Area Transportation Study, 1960.

Hamburg, John, and R.L. Creighton. "Predicting Chicago's Land Use Pattern," Journal of the American Institute of Planners 26 (1959).

Harris, B.J. Linear Programming and Projecting of Land Uses. Harrisburg, PA: State Department of Highways, Penn-Jersey Transportation Study, 1962.

Harris, B.J., et al. Research on an Equilibrium Model of Metropolitan Housing and Locational Choice. Interim Report, University of Pennsylvania, Philadelphia, 1966.

Harrison, B. "Discrimination in Space: Suburbanization and Black Unemployment in Cities," In Patterns of Racial Discrimination. Von Furstenberg, Harrison, and Horowitz, eds. Cambridge: Lexington Books, 1974.

Harrison, D., Jr., and R. MacDonald. "Willingness to Pay in Boston and Los Angeles for a Reduction in Automobile-Related Pollutants." Air Quality and Automobile Emmission Control, Vol. IV: The Costs and Benefits of Automobile Control. Washington, D.C.: National Academy of Sciences, 1974.

Hartwick, P.G. and J.M. Hartwick. "Efficient Resouirce Allocation in a Multinucleated City with Intermediate Goods." Quarterly Journal of Economics 88 (1974): 340-352.

Hausman, J. and D. McFadden. "Specification Tests for the Multinomial Logit Model." Econometrica 52 (1984): 1219-1240.

Hawley, Amos H. Human Ecology: A Theory of Community Structure. New York: Ronald Press, 1950.

Herbert, J. and B.H. Stevens. "A Model for the Distribution of Residential Activity in Urban Areas." Journal of Regional Science 2 (1960): 21-36.

Hill, D.M. "A Growth Allocation Model for the Boston Region." Journal of the American Institute of Planners 31 (1965): 111-120.

Hill, D.M., D. Brand, and W.B. Hansen. "Prototype Development of a Statistical Land Use Model for the Greater Boston Region." Highway Research Record 114 (1966): 51-70.

Hoyt, Homer. The Structure and Growth of Residential Neighborhoods in American Cities. Washington, D.C.: U.S. Government Printing Office, 1939.

Huff, David. "Ecological Transactions in Consumer Behavior." Papers and Proceedings, Regional Science Association 7 (1961): 19-28.

Hurd, Richard M. Principals of City Land Values. New York: National Bureau of Economic Research, 1972.

Ingram, K. Gregory, John F. Kain and J.R. Ginn. The Detroit Prototype of the NBER Urban Simulation Model. New York: National Bureau of Economic Research, 1972.

Johnson, N. and S. Kotz. Distributions in Statistics - Continuous Univariate Distributions. Vols. 1, 2. New York: Wiley, 1970.

Isard, Walter. Methods of Regional Analysis: An Introduction to Regional Science. Cambridge, Mass: MIT Press, 1960.

Isard, Walter. "Spatial Interaction: Some Suggestive Thoughts from General Relativity Physics." Papers and Proceedings, Regional Science Association, Vol. 27, 1971.

Kain, John F. "Housing Segregation, Negro Employment, and Metropolitan Decentralization." Quarterly Jouirnal of Economics 82 (1968): 175-197.

Kain, John F. "Housing Market Discrimination and Negro Employment," In Essays on Urban Spatial Structure. Cambridge: Ballinger, 1975.

Kain, John F., and William C. Apgar. Housing and Neighborhood Dynamics: A Simulation Study. Cambridge, MA: Harvard University Press, 1985.

Kain, John F., William C. Apgar, and J.R. Ginn. "Simulation of the Market Effects of Housing Allowances. Vol I: Description of the NBER Model." Harvard University, Kennedy School of Government, Program in City and Regional Planning, 1977a. Research Report R77-2.

Kain, John F. and William C. Apgar. "Simulation of the Market Effects of Housing Allowances. Vol II: Baseline and Policy Simulations for Pittsburg and Chicago," Harvard University, Kennedy School of Givernment, Program in City and Regional Planning, 1977b. Research Report R77-2.

Kain, John F., and W.C. Apgar, Jr. "Market Responses to Spatially Concentrated Housing and Neighborhood Improvement Programs." Cambridge, Mass: John F. Kennedy School of Government, Research Report to the U.S. Department of Housing and Urban Development, 1981.

Kim, T.J. "Alternative Transportation Modes in an Urban Land Use Model: A General Equilibrium Approach." Journal of Urban Economics 6 (1979): 197-210.

Kobrin, Frances E., and Calvin Goldscheider. The Ethnic Factor in Family Structure and Mobility. Cambridge, Mass: Ballinger, 1978.

Lerman, Steven R. "Location, Housing, Automobile Ownership and Mode to Work: A Joint Choice Model." Transportation Research Record 610 (1977).

Lieberson, Stanley. Ethnic Patterns in American Cities. New York: Free Press, 1963.

Linneman, P., and P. Graves. "Migration and Job Change: a Multinomial Logit Approach." Journal of Urban Economics 14 (1983): 263-279.

Lippman, S., and McCall, J. "The Economics of Job Search: A Survey." Economic Inquiry 14 (1976):155-189, 347-368.

Little, A.D. Community Renewal Planning. New York: Frederick A. Praeger, 1966.

Lowry, Ira. A Model of Metropolis. Santa Monica: Rand Corporation, 1964. Research Memorandum No. 4035.

Luce, R.D. Individual Choice Behavior: A Theoretical Analysis. New York: Wiley, 1959.

Luce, R.D., and P. Suppes. "Preference, Utility, and Subjective Probability." In Handbook of Mathematical Psychology, Vol 3, R. Luce, R. Bush, and E. Galanter, eds. New York: Wiley, 1965.

McCall, J.J. "Economics of Information and Job Search." Quarterly Journal of Economics 84 (1970):113-126.

McFadden, Daniel. "Conditional Lofit Analysis and Qualitative Choice Behavior." In Frontiers in Econometrics, P. Zarembka, ed. New York: Academic Press, 1973.

McFadden, Daniel. "Conditional Logit Analysis of Qualitative Choice Behavior." In Frontiers in Econometrics. P. Zarembka, ed. New York: Academic Press, 1974.

McFadden, Daniel. "Modelling the Choice of Residential Location." In Spatial Interaction Theory and Planning Models, A. Karlqvist, et al., eds. Amsterdam: North Holland Publishers, 1978.

MacRae, C. Duncan. "Urban Housing with Discrete Structures." Journal of Urban Economics 11 (1982): 131-147.

Manski, Charles. The Analysis of Qualitative Choice. Ph.D. diss. MIT, 1973.

Marshall, S.A. The Urban Institute Housing Model: Application to South Bend, Indiana. Washington, D.C.: The Urban Institute, 1976. Working Paper 216-26.

Massey, Douglas S. "Residential Succession and Segregation: The Hispanic Case." Presented at the Annual Meeting of the Population Association of America, Washington, D.C., March, 1981a.

Massey, Douglas S. "Social Class and Ethnic Segregation." American Sociological Review. 46 (1981b): 641-650.

Mills, Edwin S. "An Aggregative Model of Resource Allocation in a Metropolitan Area." American Economic Review 57 (1967): 197-210.

Mills, Edwin S. Studies in the Structure of the Urban Economy. Baltimore: Johns Hopkins, 1972a.

Mills, Edwin S. "Markets and Efficient Resource Allocation in Rural Areas." Swedish Journal of Economics 74 (1972b): 100-113.

Mills, Edwin S. "Open Housing Laws as a Stimulus to Central City Employment." Journal of Urban Economics 17 (1985): 184-188.

Mills, Edwin S., and Bruce W. Hamilton. Urban Economics. Glenview, Ill.: Scott Foresman and Company, 1984.

Mills, Edwin S., and Richard Price. "Metropolitan Suburbanization and Central City Problems." Journal of Urban Economics 15 (1984): 1-17.

Mooney, J. "Housing Segregation, Negro Employment, and Metropolitan Decentralization: An Alternative Perspective." Quarterly Journal of Economics (1969): 299-311.

Muth, Richard F. Cities and Housing. Chicago: University of Chicago Press, 1969.

Muth, Richard F. Urban Economic Problems. New York: Harper & Row, 1975.

Nelli, Humbert S. Italians in Chicago 1880-1930: A Case Study in Ethnic Mobility. New York: Oxford University Press, 1970.

Offner, P., and D. Saks. "A Note on John Kain's 'Housing Segregation, Negro Employment, and Metropolitan Decentralization'." Quarterly Journal of Economics (1971): 147-160.

Ozanne, L. and J. Vanski. Rehabilitating Central City Housing: Simulations with the Urban Institute Housing Model. Washington, D.C.: The Urban Institute, 1980. Contract Report 266-01.

Park, Robert E. "The City: Suggestions for the Investigation of Human Behavior in an Urban Environment." The American Journal of Sociology. 20 (1916): 577-612.

Park, Robert E. "The Urban Community as a Spatial Pattern and a Moral Order." In Ralph H. Turner, ed. Robert Park on Social Control and Collective Behavior. Chicago: The University of Chicago Press, 1967.

Peat, Marwick, Mitchell, and Co. "EMPIRIC", Activity Allocation Model: Applications to the Washington Metropolitan Region. Washington, D.C.: Metropolitan Washington Council of Governments, 1972.

Putman, Stephen H. Laboratory Testing of Predictive Land Use Models. Washington, D.C.: U.S. Department of Transportation, Office of Systems Analysis and Information, 1976. DOT-P-5010.

Putman, Stephen H. Integrated Analysis of Metropolitan Transportation and Location. Washington, D.C.: U.S. Department of Transportation, Office of Transportation Economic Analysis, 1980. DOT-P-30-80-32.

Putman, Stephen H. Integrated Urban Models. London: Pion Limited, 1983.

Quigley, John. "Housing Demand in the Short Run: An Analysis of Polytomous Choice." In Explorations in Economic Research, S.D. Winter, ed., Vol. 3, No. 1, 1976.

Ridker, R.G. Economic Costs of Air Pollution: Studies in Measurement. New York: Praeger, 1967.

Rose-Ackerman, S. "Racism in Urban Spatial Structure," Journal of Urban Economics 2 (1975): 85-103.

Schwartz, A. "Interpreting the Effects of Distance on Migration." Journal of Political Economy 81 (1973): 1153-1167.

Senior, M.L. "Residential Location." In A.G. Wilson, et al., eds. Models of Cities and Regions: Theoretical and Empirical Developments. Chichester: John Wiley and Sons, 1977.

Sheffi, Y. Transportation Network Equilibrium with Discrete Choice Models. Ph.D. diss., MIT, 1978.

Shevky, E. and Bell, W. Social Area Analysis. Berkeley: university of Californai Press, 1955.

Shukla, Vibhooti and PaulL Waddell. "Firm location and land use in discrete urban space: a study of the spatial structure of Dallas-Fort Worth." Regional Science and Urban Economics, Vol. 21 (1991) 225-253.

Siegel, Jay. "Intrametropolitan Migration: A Simultaneous Model of Employment and Residential Location of White and Black Households." Journal of Urban Economics 2 (1975): 29-47.

Simpson, W. "A Simultaneous Model of Workplace and Residential Location Incorporating Job Search." Journal of Urban Economics 8 (1980): 330-349.

Simpson, W. "Workplace Location, Residential Location, and Urban Commuting." Urban Studies 24 (1987): 119-128.

Stewart, J.Q. "An Inverse Distance Variation for Certain Social Influences." Sience 93 (1941).

Struyk, R.J., and M.A. Turner. "The Urban Institute Housing Market Simulation Model: Revised Theory and Solution Process." Washington D.C.: The Urban Institute, 1983. Discussion Paper 3156-05-01.

Taueber, Karl E., and Alma F. Taueber. Negroes in Cities: Residential Segregation and Neighborhood Change. Chicago: Aldine Publishing Company, 1965.

Thernstrom, Stephan. The Other Bostonians: Poverty and Progress in the American Metropolis 1880-1970. Cambridge, Mass: Harvard University Press, 1973.

U.S. Bureau of the Census. Urban Transportation Planning Package, 1980 Census: Technical Documentation for Summary Tape. Washington, D.C.: U.S. Bureau of the Census, 1983.

Vanski, J. The Urban Institute Housing Model: application to Green Bay, Wisconsin. Washington D.C.: The Urban Institute, 1976. Working Paper 216-227.

Von Thhnen, J.H. Der Isolierte Staat in Beziehung auf Landwirtschaft und National`konomie. Wissenschaftliche Buchgesellschaft, Darmstadt, 1966.

Voorhees, A.M., and Associates. Application of the Urban Systems Model (USM) to a Region - North Central Texas. Arlington, TX: North Central Texas Council of Governments, 1972.

Waddell, Paul. "Exogenous workplace choice in residential location models: is the assumption valid in a multinodal metropolis?" Geographical Analysis, Vol. 25, No. 1 (1993) 65-82.

Waddell, Paul. "Multiple-worker households: balancing residential location and workplace choices." working paper, 1996.

Waddell, Paul and Vibhooti Shukla. "Employment dynamics, spatial restructuring and the business cycle", Geographical Analysis, Vol. 25, No. 1 (1993) 35-52.

Waddell, Paul and Vibhooti Shukla. "Manufacturing location in a polycentric urban area: a study in the composition and attractiveness of employment sub-centers," Geographical Analysis, Vol. 14, No. 3 (1993) 277-296.

Ward, David. Cities and Immigrants: A Geography of Change in Nineteenth Century America. New York: Oxford University Press, 1971.

Weinberg, D. "The Determinants of Intraurban Household Mobility." Regional Science and Urban Economics 9 (1979).

Wheaton, W., Jr. "Linear Programming and Locational Equilibrium: The Herbert-Stevens Model Revisited," Unpublished Paper, MIT and University of Pennsylvania, 1974.

White, Michael J. "Racial and Ethnic Succession in Four Cities." Urban Affairs Quarterly. 20 (1984): 165-183.

Williams, H.C.W.L. "On the Formation of Travel Demand Models and Economic Evaluation Measures of User Benefit." Environment and Planning A 9 (1977): 285-344.

Wilson, A.G. "A Statistical Theory of Spatial Distribution Models." Transportation Research 1 (1967): 253-269.

Wilson, A.G. Urban and Regional Models in Geography and Planning. London: John Wiley and Sons, 1974.

Yinger, John. "An Analysis of Discrimination by Real Estate Brokers." Institute for Research on Poverty, University of Wisconsin, Madison, 1975. Discussion Paper No. 252-75.

Yinger, John. "Racial Prejudice and Racial Residential Segregation in an Urban Model" Journal of Urban Economics 3 (1976): 383-396.

Yinger, John. "Prejudice and Discrimination in the Urban Housing Market." In Current Issues in Urban Economics, ed. Peter Mieszkowski and Mahlon Straszheim. Baltimore: The Johns Hopkins University Press, 1979.